APPOINTED FOR GROWTH

Mowbray Parish Handbooks

An ABC for the PCC: A Handbook for Church Council Members, *3rd edition*
    John Pitchford
Adult Way to Faith: A Practical Handbook with Resources to Photocopy
    Peter Ball
Appointed for Growth: A Handbook of Ministry Development and Appraisal
    Kevin Eastell (ed.)
Handbook for Churchwardens and Parochial Church Councillors, *1989 edition*
    Kenneth Macmorran, E. Garth Moore and T. Briden
Handbook of Parish Finance, *3rd edition*
    Phyllis Carter and Michael Perry
Handbook of Parish Worship, *revised edition*
    Michael Perry
Handbook of Pastoral Work, *revised edition*
    Michael Hocking
Handbook of Sick Visiting
    Norman Autton
Yours, Lord: A Handbook of Christian Stewardship
    Michael Wright

In preparation
Spring into Action: A Handbook of Local Fundraising
    Martin Field and Alison Whyte (eds)
Learning for Life: A Handbook of Adult Religious Education
    Yvonne Craig

APPOINTED FOR GROWTH

A HANDBOOK OF MINISTRY
DEVELOPMENT AND APPRAISAL

Edited by Kevin Eastell

MOWBRAY

Mowbray
A Cassell imprint
Villiers House, 41/47 Strand, London WC2N 5JE
387 Park Avenue South, New York 10016–8810

First published 1994

British Library Cataloguing-in-Publication Data
A catalogue record for this book is available from the British Library.

Library of Congress Cataloging-in-Publication Data
Applied for.

ISBN 0–264–67302–6

Typeset by Colset Private Limited
Printed and bound in Great Britain by
Biddles Ltd, Guildford and King's Lynn

Contents

Foreword

There can be few more pressing needs in the church of today than the provision of adequate and appropriate support for those called to the ordination ministry.

It was this concern which encouraged me, here in Liverpool, to develop a comprehensive 'triangle of support' including not just appraisal but joint work consultation and spiritual direction.

Today's clergy, women and men, are under increasing pressure both from those in their congregations and from the wider communities they serve. Expectations, whether appropriate or not, are high and it is all too easy to be lured into an attitude of uncritical and unreflective 'activism'.

I believe all who exercise an ordained ministry in the Church of God need, somehow, to keep alive and foster the vision, excitement and challenge that fuelled their vocation; ministerial review and appraisal ought to be a non-threatening, yet supportive and creative way of doing just this, ensuring that we remain effective disciples all our lives.

I am encouraged by the publication of this book and warmly commend it to all concerned with the pastoral care, development and support of today's clergy.

✠ David Liverpool
August 1993

The Contributors

Geoffrey Babb is Director for Continuing Ministerial Education in the diocese of Manchester.

Wesley Carr is Dean of Bristol.

Peter Crick is Adviser for Continuing Ministerial Education to the Bishop of Durham.

Kevin Eastell is Director for Professional Ministry in the diocese of London.

Richard Seed is vicar of Boston Spa, near Wetherby, in the archdiocese of York.

Elizabeth Shedden is Director for Lay Ministry in the diocese of London.

Jeremy Walsh is the Bishop of Tewkesbury.

Trevor Willmott is the Director of Ordinands and Post-Ordination Training in the diocese of Peterborough.

I am the true vine, and my Father is the gardener. Any branch of mine that is barren he cuts away; and any fruiting branch he prunes clean, to make it more fruitful still. You are already clean because of the word I have spoken to you. Dwell in me, as I in you. No branch can bear fruit by itself, but only if it remains united with the vine; no more can you bear fruit, unless you remain united with me.

(John 15.1–4)

Human nature is not a machine to be built after a model, and set to do exactly the work prescribed for it; but a tree, which requires to grow and develop itself on all sides, according to the tendency of the inward forces which make it a living thing.

(from John Stuart Mill, *On Liberty*)

Introduction

KEVIN EASTELL

Throughout the history of the Church, the experience of change has brought fundamental modifications to belief and practice. Inevitably this has profoundly affected the ministers of the Church. Clearly change involves uncertainty, and clergy of all denominations are currently having to face a lot of soul searching as the Church approaches the end of the second millennium. At a time when variable expressions of ministerial provision are being explored; when financial constraint is being experienced at all levels; when deployment issues present great problems and many questions are being posed about appropriate patterns of training and education, clergy can be left with a feeling that many former points of security have been lost.

We can, however, take comfort from the fact that part of the genius of the ordained ministry is its capacity to modify its work practices to match the hour. This handbook provides a focus for one of the areas in which a realistic attempt has been made to assist clergy to understand their changing circumstances, and addresses the growing interest that has been shown in ministerial development with a process of appraisal and review.

Why has 'appraisal' been promoted? The practice of ministerial review has emerged strongly within the Churches

1

over the past fifteen years. Several explanations can be advanced to account for the growth of interest in this process. Clergy themselves have appreciated the benefits of such a process and many clergy now see as part of their personal development the services of a regular interview with a work consultant. The promotion of various schemes brings this phenomenon of individual voluntarism within the organizational structure of the Church concerned. There has also been a blossoming awareness of the professionalism of the clergy in a society where review programmes are identified with distinctive work practices.

The encouragement of such schemes within the dioceses may further have something to say about the way in which bishops and senior personnel operate in today's Churches. Many clergy will recall the days when bishops appeared to regard remoteness as an asset. Once a clergyman had been inducted he was left to get on with the job. The bishop made an annual pastoral visit to administer confirmation and generally show an interest in the parish. The archdeacon's visitation also provided an annual opportunity to enquire into the administration of the parish and its buildings.

In recent years the episcopacy has become much more managerial in its identity, and the way bishops have been enthusiastic in promoting schemes by which they can have regular interviews with their clergy is a clear demonstration of that changing identity. The workload carried by our bishops and senior personnel has increased considerably in recent years, particularly with the introduction of synodical structures. However, the care of the clergy remains a core commitment for a bishop. In our managerial climate the ministerial review programme is an organized way in which bishops can demonstrate that commitment, and is consistent with the new episcopal identity.

What the handbook contains   It is very appropriate that the handbook begins by looking at the basic theological ideas which can inform a review process. Wesley Carr, the Dean of Bristol, looks at the roles which an ordained minister may be expected to fulfil and the authority which is given to be exercised by those who are the subject of review. Living responsibly with one's vocation is a theme which Wesley Carr adopts strongly and develops fully. For Anglican clergy he uses the Ordinal as a point of reference and explores the growing interest in seeing the opportunity for regular review as a means by which complementarity in ministry can be defined and exercised.

The handbook continues with an overview of the subject which seeks to identify the major influences that have contributed to our understanding of ministerial review.

In Chapter 2 I offer a summary of the basic models and approaches to appraisal which is drawn from research conducted by the Advisory Board for Ministry of the Church of England General Synod. The overview also indicates that there is a longer historical antecedent to this aspect of ministerial life than is sometimes realized and suggests that a process of ministerial review has been a regular feature of the Church's life and witness. I conclude by arguing that the time is probably right for the Church to discover its own integrity in the design that is adopted by Church institutions rather than drawing constantly from terms of reference provided by commercial interest, industry or indeed imported from other countries. An adequate understanding of ministry in context would encourage this degree of confidence and independence.

The Bishop's Adviser for Continuing Ministerial Education in Durham, Peter Crick, addresses the question: 'How can a person get the best out of the opportunities that ministerial review offers?' He examines the issues of attitude, discipleship, relationships and objectives. He also looks at the interview process, in which he suggests an approach that a participant may adopt to maximize the effectiveness of the experience.

A work of this nature must address problems and limitations, and this task is given to Geoffrey Babb, the Director for Continuing Ministerial Education in the diocese of Manchester. Addressing the basic question of accountability, he offers a frank discussion about the limitations which obtain in attempting to conduct a ministerial review programme in a complex organization like the Church. Geoffrey also examines some of the hidden agendas which may be present in institutional schemes and the threat posed by these elements. The examination includes points of weakness which may obtain, not only with participants, but also with providers.

The perception of the clergy about participation in an appraisal scheme is explored by a parish priest. Richard Seed, vicar of Boston Spa near Wetherby in the archdiocese of York, brings to his reflections the added bonus of considerable research in the field. Previously explored issues are developed in his study from the practitioner's viewpoint. Hopes, fears and outcomes are discussed and anyone involved in conducting the ministerial review process would benefit from a careful study of this particular chapter. A specific contribution of this chapter is to explore the relationship between the person, the community in which he or she works and others to whom the person relates as a focus for ministerial review.

What is often not fully appreciated is the extent to which systems of review are extending within the Church to areas of ministry other than those being exercised by the ordained ministry. For many years the Methodist, United Reformed and Non-Conformist Churches have known the meaning of shared ministry. The Second Vatican Council recognized a more comprehensive definition of the People of God in seeing a clear relationship between the witness and work of ordained, religious and lay ministries. The Papal Encyclical *Lumen Gentium* reinforced this position by referring to *Christifideles* (followers of Christ in faithfulness), and sees the integration of all ministries within the life of the Church as an expression of *koinōnia*, partnership. The Church of England has also in recent years explored more fully the implications of complementarity in ministry. Therefore, it is refreshing to introduce into this handbook insights drawn from the lay person's perception. Elizabeth Shedden, Director for Lay Ministry in the diocese of London, writes to this brief and extends the boundary of this study by investigating how professional review is increasingly being used to assist the ministry of lay workers in the Church.

It frequently falls upon the initiative and responsibility of bishops, archdeacons and senior staff to conduct the appraisal interview. Bishop Jeremy Walsh of Tewkesbury offers some thoughts about a distinctive scheme which he pioneered in the diocese of Gloucester. He also seeks to explore how the bishop or his delegate perceives the advantages of appraisal and what the adoption of such schemes has to say about the bishop's perceptions of his *episkopē*.

The handbook concludes with an investigation into the spiritual dimension of appraisal. This investigation is provided by Trevor Willmott, Director of Ordinands and Post-Ordination Training in the diocese of Peterborough, who makes some interesting observations about the way in which clergy work and the view of God which is reflected in our work and assessment patterns.

How is the handbook arranged? Each chapter can stand as a piece of reading material in its own right, to which the reader can refer, and addresses a specific dimension of the review process. The approach which has been adopted is broadly perspectival and thereby encourages us to view both the advantages and limitations of appraisal comprehensively. Inevitably it is to be expected that basic themes will recur, but the recurrence is hopefully rescued from repetitiveness by the quality of observation which is made by the contributors. By comparing and contrasting the analyses which are offered in the handbook, the reader is led to appreciate and understand more fully the complexity of a process which involves a rich variety of considerations.

A question of title? Considerable difficulty has been experienced in designating an appropriate title for the process which is now offered in many Churches and most dioceses of the Church of England. The focus of the process is increasingly being given to the *ministerial development* of the participants. The means by which this focus is achieved is by various methods of *review* which are employed.

In many situations the process is called an *appraisal* and in some ways this is appropriate. If the process is designed to value the work that is being done by the minister; to estimate positively the contribution that a participant's ministry is making and to praise the professional commitment which may be present, then *appraisal* is a good title to give to the process, and this is very much the definition which we would seek here. However, we cannot ignore recent developments which have taken place in industry, education and the medical profession by which appraisal may be used to monitor performance and condition other factors such as remuneration and career prospects. This has served to confer upon the title certain negative features with which, I am sure, clergy would not wish to be associated.

The advertising world works very much on the principle that if you cannot sell a product, change the label. Finding a name which can universally describe the process has proved to be very evasive. In this handbook we have extensively used both *ministerial review* and *appraisal* to designate the system of a regular and structured interview which explores the ministry and personal development of the clergy involved. This choice does not imply that other titles should not be used; our limited use simply provides a degree of consistency to the text.

It will be recognized that the contributors to this handbook are drawn from the ranks of those whose life and being are very much involved in organizing, providing and offering schemes of ministerial review. Each Church, circuit and diocese has a tendency to design an appraisal scheme which is thought most appropriate for its own use. With such variety, the task of providing a handbook which can adequately examine this subject has not been easy, but at least we have attempted to address themes which may be found in most of the schemes that are currently offered. As we gain increased experience in this field there will be continuing refinement and modification as the demands which are made of the Church and its ministry change. We hope that those who use this handbook may find it a useful resource which will help both the understanding and practice of ministry.

The New Testament has little to say about statistics and results; it has much to say about growth and fruitfulness. John 15.1–11 remains for me an inspiring passage which speaks much about the distinctive relationship between ourselves, our vocation, our ministry and our Lord, to whom all who are committed with particular responsibility in the service of the Church will have to ultimately account. It is not unusual for clergy to feel somewhat 'pruned' from time to time, either by the barren constraints which may be present in their working context or by the sterile aridity which is imposed upon an occupation that does not look to the world for its justification. The Church has a pressing obligation to care for its clergy who have given their lives to its service and the fruitfulness which a life in Christ implies. If our systems of review assist to stimulate the growth of the clergy into spiritual, professional and ministerial maturity they will have achieved much. Certainly our expressions of clergy care should reflect this maturation as its intrinsic motive.

Kevin Eastell

1

Theological Insights

WESLEY CARR

To some people concern over the accountability and appraisal of parochial and other clergy seems, as with many aspects of today's Church, to result from pressure from the modern world. Hitherto, so the argument goes, it has been enough for the minister to believe that he is appraised both now and in the future by God, to whom alone he is accountable. Questions of accountability, therefore, whether to bishops or archdeacons as 'line managers' or to the lay people with whom the minister works as 'collaborative colleagues in the congregation', have seemed inappropriate. This fundamental discussion as to whether any form of clergy review is appropriate may itself be one of the factors which contribute to the difficulties that have been experienced in devising appropriate methods of appraisal. But the problem also indicates that however competent appraisers may be and however efficient the system devised, anything which is done in the Christian Church, not least with Christian ministers, is eventually justified by its theological basis.

There is, and has been for some years, considerable ferment in the theology of the ordained ministry. Overall, the tendency has been to minimize its significance. However, there may be signs of the beginnings of a recovery of confidence in such a distinctive ministry in the Church of England. The report *The Theology of the Ordained*

Ministry,[1] for instance, affirms such a particular ministry and, even more significantly, argues that it has theological significance, even if what precisely this is might not necessarily be agreed by all. There is in addition another background issue. Thinking about the ordained ministry as a topic of theological concern is usually located within the realm of ecclesiology. One outcome of the ecumenical discussions which have gone on throughout this century has been a renewed focus on this discipline. But now we may be observing a turning away from the possibly excessive enthusiasm for ecclesiology which has marked recent Church life and theological activity. Adrian Hastings, discussing the Church's authority in matters of ministry, rightly remarks:

> Ecclesiologically, it is not wrong because it has not been done before. Ecclesiologically, it is not wrong because the *orbis terrarum* has not yet pronounced on it. Ecclesiologically, it would be wrong, after such a process, to be afraid to act for no other reason than that the universal Church remains partly uncertain, partly opposed. The rightness of the particular decision must be hammered out pastorally, christologically, soteriologically, anthropologically, *but not ecclesiologically*.[2]

The temptation, therefore, is to over-elaborate the theology of something which is essentially practical and functional, namely the review of clergy ministry. It might, given suitable use of the theological imagination, be possible to embellish such work in terms of the interaction of the persons of the Trinity, a favourite preoccupation of theologians at present. Alternatively we might try to relate appraisal to the relationship between God and Jesus Christ in the working out of the incarnation, an approach which might instinctively appeal to Anglicans. Atonement theology need not be lacking: those who experience review might be inclined to attach this to the pain, suffering and death of crucifixion. But to do any of these would be both to pervert the significance of the enterprise itself and to be guilty of theological hyperbole. For, as Michael Jacobs rightly perceives,

9

It is, of course, not possible to write a theology of appraisal, but theology can inform appraisal, just as theology informs pastoral care and counselling.[3]

What I therefore wish to do in this chapter is to address some theological ideas in relation to the following premise upon which any system and practice of review is based: accountability is a function of role. This means that if anyone occupies a particular role, whatever that may be, accountability is an integral part of that role. And such accountability is the key to any scheme of review or appraisal. We may identify three principal roles that any ordained minister occupies: minister, priest, vicar.

Minister   In common with all Christians, the ordained minister has a vocation. The distinctive vocation to ordination is one among many possibilities. The Church has generally taught this, and it has recently been a prominent stance. At times in history ordination has been treated as if it were a superior vocation. But few would try to uphold such a view today. The recovery of the role of lay people individually and the laity collectively is one of today's major developments in Church life. The Christian Church is not in the business of evaluating vocations in terms of any intrinsic significance. But whatever his or her vocation, each Christian, as part of knowing to what he or she is called, needs some self-awareness. They need to be to some degree sensitized to their personal proclivities. Moreover, anyone whose ministry is chiefly exercised with other people needs such knowledge in order to be able to function at all. This is publicly recognized, for instance, in the training of therapists and social workers. But it is no less true of ordained ministers. In order to work at all, whether with individuals or more often with groups, such as meetings and congregations, they need a basic level of self-awareness. However, the quality and extent of a minister's self-perception cannot become the criterion against which the activity and ministry of an ordained person is to be reviewed or evaluated. It is likely that self-knowledge will follow the process of review, but it is not the primary purpose.

When ministry is considered in terms of a person's vocation the focus falls upon responsibility. The sort of question to be asked is: How am I acting with the authority that God has given me, whether as an ordained minister, a dustman, a teacher, a solicitor, or to whatever I believe that I have been called? In other words, the scrutiny of anyone's vocation is to what extent it is genuinely to be perceived as a divine call or to what extent it is personal prejudice masquerading as such? But such questions are those that ultimately individuals can only answer for themselves. A process of review and evaluation will assist, but it cannot be the distinctive means of acquiring self-knowledge. Nor can such acquisition be the aim of such a process.

Living responsibly with one's vocation brings to the fore the theological criterion of faithfulness. The Gospel invitation is to be faithful to one's calling. In practical terms this draws our attention to duty, both a sense of it and the way in which we carry it out. It is here that the current emphasis on the ministerial theme of the servant is best accommodated. The minister as servant is a widely assumed basis for ministry. But this concept of 'servant' then tends to become a catch-all, covering almost anything that the minister wishes. The twin notions of faithfulness and duty, however, sharpen our concept of the servant. The brief parable of the unprofitable servant in Luke 17.7ff. is illuminating. It describes how the master may legitimately hold unlimited expectations of his servant. And this is matched by the servant's responsibility not to limit his duties: 'When you have done all, you should say, "We are unworthy servants; we have only done that which it is our duty to do".' The twin themes of duty and obedience are in this story brought together in a way which undergirds the idea of the minister's personal review of his or her self-knowledge. To what extent is he or she sustaining duty to God? Such a question is partially answered, for instance, by reference to the saying of the Office. The minister's spirituality is marked by *officium*, that is, duty. Thus, we are given an external test of the continuing spirituality of the minister. Or we might add that the ordained minister is distinguished by Holy Orders. It is possible to check to what extent a minister is able to take these up and live with them by allowing them to give structure to his or her life. There are such external tests of the minister, but inevitably concern with vocation will tend towards the person as much as, or even more than, the role.

Priest The word 'priest' has always been controversial in the Church of England, possibly as much now as at any time previously. The issue of the ordination of women to the priesthood has again exposed profound differences within the Church over the meaning of this ministry. The word 'priest' is accepted by some and rejected by others. There is, however, whatever word is used, a widespread recognition that those who are ordained carry a significant representative and public role. It is the ordained ministers' responsibility to speak both *for* and *to* the Christian congregation. On the one hand, they articulate *for* the congregation the word of God as this emerges through the life of the congregation and its members, though clergy who claim to exercise an 'enabling ministry' are often directing people more than they may acknowledge. On the other hand, there is also a way in which the ordained minister offers the possibility of God *to* a congregation. He or she speaks not only from within the community but is also invited, and expected, to speak to it from an alternative, outside perspective. When this activity is corrupted into a belief that the priest mediates God to the congregation the controversies start. But the ordained minister is specifically engaged in a 'priestlike task'. These words come from Keats's poem 'Bright Star':

The moving waters at their priestlike task
Of pure ablution round earth's human shores.[4]

The role of the priest is to be one on whom public expectations are focused. He or she is caught up in a pastoral ministry of refreshment and cleansing (care and absolution) among the everyday human activities not only of the congregation but of people at large – 'earth's human shores'. However, around this concept of 'priest' the theology of the ordained ministry and what is involved in a review of ministry today come into conflict. The problem is not practical: it derives from different views of the nature of the ordained ministry. The two Ordinals of the Church of England illuminate the issue.

The Ordinal of 1662, in common with the rest of that book, largely assumes a Christian world. It tends to identify the congregation and society, or at least not to differentiate them too strongly. But the Order for the Ordination of Priests nevertheless includes an acknowledgement that such an identification is not complete. The bishop's charge includes the sentence:

> [You are] to seek for Christ's sheep that are dispersed abroad, and for his children who are in the midst of this naughty world, that they may be saved through Christ for ever.

In other words, the core of the priest's role is mission to and concern for a public which lies outside the present bounds of the Church. They may be potential or implicit Christians, but they are not just now included within the congregation. This attitude contrasts strongly with that in the Alternative Service Book of 1980, which omits this aspect of priestly ministry. There is no reference to anything beyond caring for the people of God, by which clearly is meant the local congregation. There is, therefore, a crucial difference: the Ordinal under which nearly all priests are being ordained today is more congregational than parochial, more concerned with enabling and therefore collaborative ministry than with differentiation and therefore complementary ministry.

The distinction between collaborative and complementary gives clarity to ministry and, therefore, to what ₁eview of ministry implies for the theology of ministry. There is much talk today of collaborative ministry. The term describes the way in which the clergy and the laity, within the setting of a congregation, can and should work together. The model of the Church which is usually invoked to justify this belief is that of the Body of Christ. The way in which it works out tends towards the notion that every member of the congregation has a ministry, among which that of the ordained is merely one. The clergy involved are inclined to see themselves as paid or authorized officers of the organization (or, for some, organism) of the congregation. In some ways the collaborative approach to ministry is a response to excessive clericalism of the Church. But more significantly it is also an internal, domestic view. In other words, it is a way of conceiving the Church and its overall ministry which derives from within. Its theological undergirding derives from the indicative statement repeated in the Eucharist: 'We are the Body of Christ.'

By contrast, the idea of complementary ministry assigns distinctive roles to the ordained and to the laity not because these are expected or demanded from within the Church, but because they enable the Church to operate more effectively in its social context outside. This concept of the Church is negotiated between those who believe that they are Christ's representatives and those among whom the Church exists and exercises its ministry who have expectations as to what it should be. The Body of Christ from this perspective is continually being created as what others believe and look for, and is negotiated by the Christian Church in relation to what it believes it is itself called to be. To further that mission, the Church offers the world two specific access points. There is, firstly, the ministry of Christian people, who, whatever their testimony, claim the authority of their experience. Their witness is essentially like that of the man born blind in John 9: 'This one thing I know: once I was blind, now I can see' (John 9.25). And there is, secondly, the complementary authority of authorized representation. For some purposes, if people are to discover access to God they need to have access to someone who they have reason to believe can speak to them with distinctive religious authority. His or her message cannot be personal testimony alone: it must be that mixture of Scripture, tradition and reason which has to be articulated in specific moments of people's lives. It is for such ministry that people have reason to look to the ordained person, to whom the Church publicly assigns such a role. Neither ordained nor lay ministry is superior to the other, but in terms of people's approach to God through the Church's ministry they are complementary.

This distinction is further brought out when we consider the priest's authority. In the old Ordinal the bishop gives priests many warnings, and then at the ordination includes the prayer:

> So that as well by these thy ministers, as by them *over whom they shall be appointed thy ministers*, thy holy name may be for ever glorified. (My italics)

But this idea of differentiated activity and authority over others is missing from the new Ordinal. This stresses a vague sense of collaboration, getting on together, rather than the much clearer concept of complementarity. The theological question here is of great significance. It is not about working models of the Church but about what lies behind them: on what basis do we construct models of the Church? We might now legitimately invoke the doctrine of the Trinity, within which, so far as classical theory argues, divine activity is necessarily complementary rather than collaborative. Not only are the persons differentiated, but more particularly the activities of God the Trinity cannot be divided. We believe that the activities of the members of the Trinity are always complementary. Any divine activity, therefore, including that which is in human experience mediated through the ministry of clergy and lay people, will also carry the same identifying mark.

The idea of ministerial complementarity can be related to work achievement and consequently to appraisal. It is, for example, possible to assess to what extent the differentiated activity of the minister in his or her priestly role is complementary to that of those with whom he or she works in their distinctively lay roles. The notion of complementarity draws attention to roles and therefore makes assessment possible. By contrast, the idea of collaboration softens differences in favour of mutuality and joint activity. As a result of this it is difficult to know precisely the focal point for the assessment. It may be, therefore, that the demand for assessment and evaluation is in fact inconsistent with trends in the theology of ordination. Appraisal against the description of priesthood in the new Ordinal is difficult because of the changed assumptions that it portrays.

That, however, does not prevent consideration of the role of priest as a point for review. When we think of priestly ministry, whether that of the great High Priest, Christ himself, or the role of priest in the Church's ministry, we are directed to the issue of holiness. This word describes the distinctive presence and lifestyle of the public minister as representative of God or the Church – that is, priest. We may expect priests to be holy people. But holiness is not so much an intrinsic quality of individuals; that would make it an impossible ideal. Developing personal self-awareness, which comes with growth and maturity, will enlarge the concept of holiness and consequently make it seem less and less attainable. Holiness is not a possession or a personal attribute so much as something assigned. It is what others expect of the priest. In other words, whenever we confront the role of priest we address the question of expectation.

The theological basis on which we might attempt assessment of what is expected is simple to see: it is the notion of

God as judge. Divine judgement according to the Christian tradition is both awesome and merciful. It is awesome because it puts the judged person in a complementary relationship to the judge: all that is done lies open not just for its own sake but also for what it says about the beliefs concerning the judge himself. The idea that God judges has suffered from over-extension of the judicial metaphor, not least in the crude way that this has sometimes been used in the theology of the atonement. Yet the concept of judge within the Christian tradition derives from the Jewish notion of ruler or, as we might say using the language of the 1662 Ordinal, a God who is appointed over us. Such judgement must always be ultimate. The question, however, for the review of the role of priest is how it is to be made proximate. It seems possible to have a theological approach to evaluation which is consonant with the idea of divine judgement, so long as in practice the distinctive role of priest as focus of expectations rather than of intrinsic merit is addressed. The forms which the question takes is: 'To what extent does this person represent Christ?' That is an awesome question of holiness. But when asked, it proves to be not just a question to the ordained person. It brings to the fore in the Church's life an investigation into what theological perspective it holds on all human life.

Divine judgement is also awesome in that it frightens. If the notion of God is awe-inspiring, any idea of what we are in relation to God arouses appropriate anxiety. But we have discovered that fear of God is not the same as terror. It is rather, as the Psalmist calls it, the beginning of wisdom (Psalm 111.10). 'Wisdom' in the context of review and appraisal might today mean that the process of making an evaluative judgement about anyone is an acting out of the way that we experience the presence of God in his world. Again, therefore, the theological approach to the process of review and assessment leads to a more profound understanding of the nature of the Church. This is the way in which we ultimately offer a theological justification of the appraisal and assessment of the clergy. It is not firstly a matter of whether it will benefit them. For any benefit so far as ordained ministers are concerned must be assessed on the Christian model. This is always determined by others. The relevant theme is that of 'for the sake of others', expressed in the Greek preposition *hyper*. So in specifically appraising someone in the role of priest, we create a process of scrutiny which, while benefiting the minister, is of even more value to others. Such an approach is theologically justified by Christ's own ministry for (*hyper*) others and by the test of the incarnation/atonement nexus of doctrine.

Vicar Discussions about today's ministry are many and varied. But as far as people are concerned the world of the Church of England is populated by three types of individuals: bishops, vicars, and not-vicars. Whatever a person's precise orders or ministry, he or she will usually be thought of as 'Vicar'. The most junior curate discovers that when he walks down the street in a dog collar he is assumed to be a vicar. The same is true of a woman deacon.[5] This role is the underlying model of most authorized ministries in the Church of England. And whilst it has been subject to much scrutiny and under a certain amount of attack, the role of vicar remains for many the point of association with the Church. For instance, the most extreme Evangelicals meet their Catholic colleagues precisely at this point: they may have little in common in their beliefs about the Church or even about the Gospel, but they are united in that they are both perceived as vicars (and probably equally perceived as eccentric).

The role of vicar is important in the Church of England, because it defines a distinctive theology of ministry which arises from a particularly English ecclesiology. It also highlights a fundamental differentiation which, if lost, has a deleterious effect on the life of the Church. This is the distinction between 'parochial' and 'congregational'. We have already noted today's tendency in the Church of

England to drift towards congregationalism which expresses itself in the assumption that the public minister is called to work with and enable a Christian congregation. That is undoubtedly true, but it is insufficient as a definition of what the ordained minister is about.

The difference at this point between the responsibility of the vicar and that of the congregation is expounded at an Institution when the bishop says: 'Receive this cure of souls, which is both yours and mine.' In giving this charge, the bishop makes the vicar answerable for the cure of souls in the *parish* – that is, he has a responsibility to minister to, with and for all the people in his parish, even if he has little or nothing to do with some of them. This is not so much a matter of statistics and practical attention as a set of the mind: the vicar's assumptive thinking and stance are to be first and foremost parish-orientated, not church-orientated, whatever the demands of the Church and congregation. By contrast, the congregation's task is naturally to evangelize and work in the parish area, but it is not formally limited to that. And there is no responsibility enjoined upon lay Christians with their other vocations to have the cure of souls of the parish. They should be, if they are fully aware of their vocation, primarily occupied elsewhere in living and proclaiming the Christian Gospel.

The 'cure of souls' is not simply another way of describing pastoral care. The Latin word *cura* refers to responsibility for the eternal welfare of the whole human being. Because of this charge a vicar is required to be concerned about every aspect of human life in his or her parish. Parochial boundaries exist in order to provide a limit to the range of such human life for which he is responsible.[6] This task is always unmanageable even in the smallest parish: it could not be faced in the whole world. But the question under which the work of a minister as vicar is reviewed is always that of whether and to what extent souls are being cured or not.

On this basis it is possible to carry out appraisal and at the same time discover the structural, pastoral and consequently the theological basis on which it is being done. Put simply, the appraiser is reviewing the parochial activity of the minister. It is sometimes said that this cannot be done without also investigating the way that he or she relates to the congregation and the overall effectiveness of that church's functioning. To some extent that is true, and the dilemma cannot be ignored. But it is not the whole case. For the congregational life, in which the vicar participates, can be audited. But such an audit is a separate function from that of appraisal of the minister.

The focus of review of a vicar's ministry, therefore, will be to what extent the bishop–vicar relationship is furthering the cure of souls in the parish. As part of that, but certainly not the whole, there would be an enquiry into the way in which the vicar–people relationship is serving the working of the Church in that place as well as serving his responsibility for the cure of souls.

Conclusion These three roles are, of course, not completely separable. But when we differentiate them we begin to discover a definable and possible process of review and appraisal. Certain theological dimensions to the life of the minister and of the Christian Church also become clearer. To summarize, therefore:

1 The role of *minister* directs our attention to each Christian's responsibility for his or her vocation. This is lived out in terms of duty, and the ordained minister has as much his or her distinctive duty as anyone else.

2 The role of *priest*, understood in a wide sense, focuses on holiness, and is lived out in the context of divine judgement and the way in which assigned authority is exercised authority.

3 The role of *vicar* is focused on the complementary nature of ministry, especially in relation to the bishop and the parish. This is tested by whether souls in the parish are

receiving the cure that becomes the vicar's responsibility through licensing and installation.

Appraisal or review of ministry, therefore, does not need a specific theological justification. Indeed, there is no 'theology of appraisal'. But it offers insights into thinking theologically about the Church's activity and the specific task of the ordained ministry. It is sometimes claimed that review will improve the quality of work of the ordained clergy. That may or may not be the case: we do not have enough experience to know. But by taking up appraisal as an assumed dimension to the life of ordained ministers we should usefully be refocusing our awareness of ecclesiological issues and putting these firmly in the realm of theological topics, rather than merely encouraging a pragmatic approach to ministry.

References

1 (Advisory Board for Ministry, London, 1990).
2 Cited in M.A.H. Melinsky, *The Shape of the Ministry* (The Canterbury Press, Norwich, 1992), p. 174; my italics.
3 Michael Jacobs, *Holding in Trust* (SPCK, London, 1989), p. 3.
4 See Wesley Carr, *The Priestlike Task* (SPCK, London, 1985).
5 On this general perception and some of its consequences see the papers in Wesley Carr (ed.), *Say One for Me* (SPCK, London, 1992).
6 See Wesley Carr, 'Working with dependency and keeping sane' in *The Parish Church?*, ed. G. Ecclestone (Mowbray, London and Oxford, 1988), pp. 109ff.

2

Survey of Current Use

KEVIN EASTELL

Those who are ordained have always, to a greater or lesser extent, been seen to work in relationship with each other. Part of our belonging in the wider Church context implies that we do not work in isolation and the ecclesiastical structures in which we operate encourage us as clergy to see our ministry as contributing something to the greater whole. We receive our ordination as deacons and priests at the hands of our bishops, with the consent of the gathered Christian community, and the character of the Orders we receive is outlined within the terms of the Ordinal. Appropriately, the contribution of the ordained ministry is expected to complement other ministries within the People of God. These issues are covered more fully elsewhere in this handbook, but the main observation one would wish to make at this point is that ordained ministry in the Church of England or any other Church affiliation cannot be viewed as being a ministry conducted in individual isolation.

It may also be observed that the prospect of individual clergy reviewing their ministerial practice in relationship to the wider ministry of the Church is not an innovative development of our time. The distinctive contribution of charismatic ministry was very much recognized, authorized and compared in the early Church.[1] As this charismatic phase gave way to more institutional forms, so the systems by which clergy could correlate their work were also introduced. In the High Middle Ages, for example, this correlation was expressed in the systematic visitation programmes devised by the reforming bishops of the eleventh to the thirteenth centuries. These bishops toured their vast dioceses and arrived in localities where they established their peripatetic social and legal courts and made sure that the clergy in their various Orders were performing their duties well. The work of the parochial priests, administrative deacons, liturgical acolytes and sub-deacons would be ennobled by the experience, and the archdeacons would apply appropriate justice to the dissolute, immoral and wayward clergy. The rural deans generally kept an eye on things between the visitations and maintained the bishop's brooding presence over the situation.[2] In many ways, the system which obtained at this time within the provisions of Catholicism was far more searching for those who held the 'benefit' of the clergy than anything which is offered in the provisions of the present day.

It was as an incumbent in the diocese of Liverpool in 1978 that I first engaged in ministerial review in what was then called a 'Joint Work Consultation'. The programme involved seeing one's area dean and discussing with him certain basic questions about the parish and work practices that were being adopted. It was not designed to be too intensive or intrusive but did establish a healthy contact between those of us who worked alone, and our deanery and diocese. Part of the success of the Joint Work Consultation was without doubt that it was conducted by the area dean, who by then had become virtually an elected appointment by the clergy of the deanery in that particular diocese. The area dean, therefore, was not readily identifiable with line management. He was recognized as being basically alongside the clergy and accordingly held the confidence of the chapter.[3]

Since that time, I have been regularly appraised in an evolving provision of review schemes. The Manchester scheme in the 1980s was conducted by either the area bishop or the archdeacon in what was clearly a line management model, but which was so designed that it contained a strong work consultancy element and as such proved to be an affirming and useful experience. The cumulative effect of being exposed to the influences of ministerial review and appraisal has left me favourably disposed to the process as a general practitioner in both priesthood and parochial ministry.

Influences upon ministerial review Appraisal provision in Britain generally relies heavily upon behaviourally orientated methodologies borrowed from the USA. These methodologies possess individual, psychological and self-awareness characteristics which are measured in terms of the patterns of human behaviour that are manifested. This influence has been advantageous in informing an emerging development of appraisal in the Church in the British Isles. However, the development has been to some extent restricted in the sense that it has not allowed, for example, the Church of England to evolve schemes which were more appropriate to its actual working context; a context which is of course quite different from the workings of the Episcopal Church in the United States. The models adopted in the United States possessed a strong managerial emphasis which served to encourage improved achievement levels on many fronts, including the skills, knowledge, tasks and interdisciplinary bases upon which modern ministry has been constructed. The episcopacy, particularly in the Church of England, has increasingly found itself having to manage its contact with the clergy in a structured way. Therefore, the American models were warmly received by the newly appointed bishops into their dioceses.

Further impetus was given to the development of appraisal in the Church by the emergence of evaluation systems in secular organizations. For example, the growth of this initiative in education has presented similar difficulties to those which have been experienced in the Church.[4] Possibly one of the greatest influences upon the evolution of appraisal is to be found in the research of Loren Mead in the 1970s. The framework which was eventually designed from this source is worthy of summary.[5] Mead basically approached the construct of an appraisal programme by identifying four areas of attention: the *person*, the *task*, the *performance* and the *context*.

Personal individualism A relationship clearly exists between the individual and the perceptions which are held about what it means to be an ordained minister. Pastoral ministry, therefore, has both a public and a private identity. The personal development model was identified as being important in reconciling tensions between role and person. This emphasis on personal development has been so virulent in its reception into the Church that it has dominated the educational and training patterns which have emerged in pre- and post-ordination training. Personal formation has tended to replace priestly formation and ministerial develop- ment has adopted a distinctly individualistic view in most of our training establishments. It is understandable, there- fore, that many who now devise review and appraisal schemes wish to sustain this particular emphasis. The per- sonal approach requires that individuals learn to meet posi- tively personal criticism in the pursuit of self-improvement. This approach is offered as an alternative to personal per- ceptions of failure and incompetence which may be felt by the individual and which may be left to distort the insights held about oneself and one's ministry.

Task orientation Loren Mead observed that pastoral work was essentially both variable in its practice and flexible in its operation. The tasks one performs, therefore, have to be understood from the person's perspective in contrast to the employing institution's expectations. Consequently, the methods employed in appraising the tasks of the minister

25

were to seek an assessment of defined areas of competence within ministry. For example, the 30 questions exercise of Kebie Hatcher was highly recommended. This exercise asked how important a list of 30 pastoral tasks was to those participating. The participants could be members of a congregation, the bishop, the vestry or any other interest. By correlating the results of this questionnaire, the areas of convergence and divergence between the various interests and the minister were identified. These expectations could then be related to the individual minister's competence to meet them.

Individual performance   It was recognized that levels of ministerial performance were difficult to measure. A tension was seen to exist between attempting to evaluate performance in terms of quantity (e.g. attendance, finance, confirmation candidates) and quality (how many saints has the minister produced!). It was, therefore, strongly suggested that the only real measurement which could be applied was the subjective evaluation of the individual minister and the way in which he or she saw personal performance. In assisting the process by which this perception was discovered, the emphases which individuals placed upon their work pattern were identified as being an important consideration. For example, a Kingdom/Justice orientation to one's ministry was anticipated to reveal quite different expectations in performance from those of the person who applied an administrative/worship focus to the work of ministry.

Context of operation   The place in which and the people with whom the minister worked were recognized as being germane considerations in the review of ministry. The participant was encouraged to designate the advantages and constraints which obtained in the working context and which either promoted fulfilment or frustration in ministry. Again, analytical methods were devised and offered which could identify these advantages and constraints. The analysis was seen as part of the *experiential learning* which was focused on what came to be considered as *ministry in context*. This framework, templated by the four areas of *person, task, performance* and *context* associated with ministerial review postulated by Loren Mead, continues to feature in many review schemes currently offered in the Church.

However, it should be recognized that Loren Mead posed fundamental questions about appraisal which remain as pertinent as ever. Who and what is it for? Is an appraisal to serve the purposes of the institution, the person or the profession? Clarity of intent was constantly advocated by Loren Mead, and that prerequisite remains as important as ever. Lucid aims with supportive objectives continue to be conditional for the success or failure of any programme that is devised.

Independent agencies   Those who have been involved in the Ministry Development Consultations organized by the Edward King Institute at Lincoln will also recognize the influence which Tom Brown contributed to the process of appraisal. The approach is a self-appraisal system and seeks to answer two basic questions which are frequently raised by those who are involved in continuing education. The first question is, how are clergy to be motivated without the help of institutional rewards (promotion, pay rises, increased productivity, etc.) to continue their learning? Secondly, how can clergy be helped to choose resources for learning that are most appropriate to increase their competence in particular ministerial situations?

The Institute suggests that difficulties may be experienced if the diocese or circuit itself supplies a framework to answer these questions. The distanced objectivity and confidentiality of the Ministry Development Consultation, which is specifically owned by the participants, is offered as a means of motivation and integrity in the ministerial development which is encouraged. The consultation itself is demanding and calls for a significant investment of time, prayer, thought and money from the participant. At least six hours preparation followed by usually four days residence are necessary. Perhaps the most significant characteristic of these consultation events is the support which is freely and mutually given by the participants themselves. As much as anything else in the process it is this peer group ingredient that assures the participants of their personal value and calling. The approach relies heavily upon the individual perceptions and personal development emphases which have certainly proved very useful for some, but a source of discomfort for others.

Another agency which has provided opportunities for ministerial review and development is St George's House at Windsor. Provision for those in a situation of mid-ministry review has been a feature of the St George's programme for some years now, and a direct link is established between a time for reflective review and learning. St George's is a place where clergy from all denominations can attend courses which are designed to meet the needs of the various stages in their ministerial development. The courses offered are intended to illuminate responsibilities and clarify functions in the modern context of ministry. Besides the possibilities offered at St George's, most of the theological colleges also provide facilities by means of which clergy may engage in some form of ministerial review, along with independent organizations like AVEC in London.

Needs of the institution   It may be justifiably argued that Church leadership can often interpret appraisal in terms of the management of the human resources which exist within the diocese, circuit or district. This interpretation is frequently enhanced by the hope that the skills, gifts and abilities which may be possessed by the local clergy will be discovered, recognized and affirmed. Some may even look to the review system to assist the senior staff in appointing personnel where they will be best located both for their own fulfilment and the good of the Church. The expectation may alternatively exist that the process will result in the encouragement of individuals to make the most of the situations in which they are placed and in which they may remain.

It could be suggested that interpretations of this kind remain idealistic in nature and in practice achieve only a modest degree of success. The limitations precluding these hopes being realized are numerous. For example, there are no clear goals attached to most dioceses as institutions, and they tend to be a management structure which is a confused mix of hierarchy, democracy and individual independence. Few dioceses have realistically defined strategies which look to their future condition, and which can function as reference points for their review systems.

The diocesan institution simply does not possess the usual 'carrots' and 'sticks' by means of which expectations can be delivered. Egalitarian pay scales prevent the rewards of bonus or increased salary for performance being awarded. Conversely, it is difficult to envisage what corrective measures could be applied to discovered incompetence apart from a moan in the bishop's staff meeting. Moreover, the system lacks the mobility to facilitate efficient deployment of clergy.

Occasionally these expectations on the part of a diocese may be met in individual circumstances when influences combine to work in the system's favour. But, in my view, it would be a mistake to expect that an appraisal scheme could be devised which would completely deliver the complex requirements of the diocese as an institution. Particularly, for example, as the Church of England comes to the conclusion of the twentieth century with its attendant financial, doctrinal and ministerial problems, it is going to be the case that dioceses become 'ring-fenced' with regard to clergy movements and increasingly congregationalist in character. In this situation, perhaps the hope that the review system will encourage individuals to make the most of the situation in which they are placed will be the most helpful.

Needs of the individual Loren Mead helpfully indicated that professional development emerged from two basic questions: 'How am I doing?' and 'How can what I do be improved?' The overwhelming advantage of Churches in the promotion of their appraisal schemes is the motivation of most clergy to perform to the best of their ability. Of all the professional groups, the clergy must rate highly in the motivational league table. In a very real way clergy are permanent amateurs, but 'amateurs' in the literal French sense of the word in that they do the work of their vocation for the sheer love of it. However, admitting this value does not preclude the professional application which clergy historically have brought to their work. Clergy want to become better priests or ministers, more capable managers of the Church's resources, more competent pastors, effective teachers and devoted servants of the Kingdom. Therefore, it remains vital for the success of an appraisal scheme that a climate of motivational support and trust is provided.

In the United States the reference points are frequently the congregations and vestries of parishes in which clergy serve. These interests are canvassed by the review system, and individual clergy performance is measured by the findings which emerge. However, for clergy in the Church of England, the point of reference is not only the congregation which they serve, but also the wider parish interests to which they are appointed. At this point in time the American approach would be too impractical for the clergy in England. English clergy have developed their skills within an identifiable professional group, and whereas I think that most clergy in the Church of England would find peer group assessment acceptable, they would not respond warmly to external evaluation. Within the review process it is important that individual clergy are given the opportunity to know that their ministry is being taken seriously at a professional level and that what is discovered in the review will be competently handled.

The importance of further education and in-service

training has emerged as a vital element in the review process. Consequently, an appropriate identification and designation of future training needs and educational development has been an effective way of meeting directly individual anticipation and reconciling this with institutional expectation. It is particularly fortunate that the growth of continuing ministerial education in the Church of England has been along personal and professional lines, with the emphases in *The Continuing Education of the Church's Ministry* on both skills and stages in ministry.[6] An association between ministerial review and continuing education must emerge as one of the great benefits and advantages which has arisen over the past twenty years in the Church. This development has been a feature which can be found in other Churches in the British Isles.

May 1988 in the Church of England saw the publication of a substantial report on appraisal which was titled *Ministry Development and Review*. This document was received by the Continuing Ministerial Education Committee of ACCM and was subsequently circulated to the dioceses for consideration. The report began with the observation that:

> Appraisal, or evaluation of ministry, has been, and is being, undertaken under a variety of titles in a variety of ways for a variety of purposes in more than half the dioceses of the Church of England.[7]

The terms of reference of the working group which produced the report were clear. First, to discover the rationale of what was being and is being attempted and what in practice was happening in the dioceses. Secondly, to clarify the notion of assessment and appraisal in terms of the language used; the underlying intentions which were declared and the connections with traditional spiritual disciplines which were found to be present. Thirdly, to produce a paper outlining the directions in which the Committee might proceed.

It will be recognized how seminal this paper has proved to be in informing the dioceses about how appraisal could be developed. It is a particular feature of life in the Church of England that dioceses exercise considerable autonomy in the ways in which proposals and ideas are accepted, developed and applied. However, with over twenty dioceses in 1988, and considerably more now, having adopted ministerial review schemes, it is inevitable that clusters of shared practice could be expected to emerge. Four basic models were found to be operating in the dioceses.

First, there was the annual or biennial meeting which took place between the minister and bishop or his delegate. Secondly, there were regular meetings provided for ministers with experienced colleagues who operated outside the hierarchical provisions of the diocese. Thirdly, there was the group model of clergy meeting on a regular basis and sharing the appraisal process. Finally, there was the individually based model by which the minister annually conducted a self-review by means of a checklist or questionnaire provided by the diocese. Not only did the working group describe these various models, it also usefully collated ɩhe distinctive emphases and identified the varying nature of reporting along with the advantages and disadvantages which these models possessed. As the findings of the working group defy improvement it is sufficient to represent the summary which was offered. (See pp. 34–5.)

The report went on to categorize the various schemes which were on offer in terms of their underlying assumptions. Involved in this process was the clarification of the four descriptions which have become associated with the review process and which have been employed to portray what is taking place.

1 *Ministry development programme.* Associated closely with continuing ministerial education, this title suggested a range of flexible programmes that an individual may use to assess the various stages of ministry through which he or she was proceeding.

2 *Ministerial review.* This appellation was identified within the report as a neutral term which carried perspectives of reflection upon one's work and involved the identification of both strengths and weaknesses in ministry. From this review some prognostications relating to future work patterns, skills improvement and educational development were expected to be made.

3 *Assessment.* The report suggested that the use of this term should be limited to describe the occasional need for work evaluation which was associated with a change in appointment, renewal of contract, possible retirement or even a process leading to dismissal.

4 *Parish review.* This designation was identified as being associated with, though not necessarily part of, the ministerial review approach. By incorporation it could have the advantage of giving a diocese or circuit an estimation as to how a particular parish was working and indeed was being worked by its minister. It encouraged a parish to investigate its aims and objectives as a ministerial unit and integrate the particular ministry of the incumbent with those aspirations.

A key recommendation from this paper was that budget provision should be made to support whatever scheme was adopted and that regular monitoring of the programmes should take place so that flexibility was facilitated and future modification was possible. Without doubt, the success or failure of the schemes which are promoted lies not so much in their inherent competence or motivational acceptance as in the availability of funding to secure the delivery of what is agreed, offered and provided.

More recently, a paper was produced from the CME Officers' National Conference in 1992[8] which reiterated many of the recommendations that had previously been offered in the 1988 report. Possibly the matter of primary concern which emerged from this monitoring paper was the

Method	Emphasis	Nature of reporting	Advantages	Disadvantages
A Annual or biennial meeting between minister and bishop (or experienced person appointed by bishop and trained for this work).	Episcopal responsibility for ministry in the diocese (supervision of work done and also pastoral care of clergy).	Full report on meeting kept in bishop's file, including response by minister.	1. Minister feels cared for by bishop. 2. Bishop has up-to-date information about minister and parish(es). 3. Provides outside person to work with minister concerned and help him think things through. 4. Probably more commitment to action because bishop involved. 5. Easier to challenge individual in one-to-one situation. 6. Makes clear development and training needs.	1. More hierarchical – more threatening. 2. Feelings of being inspected by bishop. 3. Might be less frank because of written report. 4. Clergy feel caught in conflict between expectations and demands of parish(es) and ideals presented by bishop. 5. Difficult for bishop and minister to handle issues of episcopal authority and pastoral care at same time. 6. May lead to unrealistic expectation about future appointments.
B Probably two meetings per year between minister and experienced colleague who has been trained for this work.	Educational. Shared analysis of individual situation so as to identify training and development needs.	Confidential. Possible short statement of agreed training plan.	1. Provides outside person to work with minister and help him think things through. 2. Confidential – therefore non-threatening. 3. More open and frank discussion. 4. Easier to challenge individual in one-to-one situation. 5. Makes clear development and training needs.	1. No information given to bishop. 2. Possibly less commitment to action because bishop not involved. 3. Uncertainty regarding structure (i.e. setting up, monitoring, promoting this kind of scheme).

Method	Emphasis	Nature of reporting	Advantages	Disadvantages
C Group of clergy meeting on a regular basis, working together and appraising each other in turn.	Group support.	Confidential to group. No other reporting.	1. Provides continuing support. 2. Insights from a variety of points of view.	1. Likely to degenerate into general discussion. 2. More difficult to challenge individuals in group setting. 3. More difficult to identify specific priorities and areas of development. 4. No information given to bishop. 5. Less commitment to action plan. 6. Difficult to set up and sustain this pattern.
D Individual minister working annually with checklist or questionnaire supplied by diocese.	Self-appraisal.	Confidential. (If report required to be returned, this method is bureaucratic.)	1. Least threatening. 2. Easy to offer to all.	1. No support from outside. 2. No sense of care. 3. Little commitment to action plan. 4. No information given to bishop. 5. Does not make clear development and training needs. 6. No guarantee the job will be done.

ad hoc way in which many of the established diocesan schemes were developing. Unclear objectives, confused aims and expectations, variable practice and incompetence were all surfacing within the findings of this paper, along with the prevailing threat of starved support brought about by financial constraint. It is hoped that the recommendations made in this 1992 report will be taken and applied seriously in the dioceses. They are as follows:

(a) That there now be a thorough study of the purpose and practice of the appraisal of Church of England clergy.
(b) That appraisal schemes have clear, limited and published objectives.
(c) That they have a clear design and structure to implement those objectives.
(d) That the identification of training needs be a principal outcome of clergy appraisal schemes.
(e) That all appraisers be properly trained and receive continuing support.

The experience which has now been acquired by the Churches in this field has encouraged the development of an independent integrity in the matter of appraisal and a diminished reliance upon models either borrowed from the secular context or imported from foreign parts. That integrity includes a greater understanding of the particular context in which ministry is conducted; an increased appreciation of the expectations of congregations and employing institutions; and an awareness of the limitations which ministry in Britain imposes. It is hoped that in the years ahead our expertise will become more refined, highly polished, precisely focused and competently applied. But the parish priest, deacon or minister will be the ultimate evaluator of the success or failure of any scheme. That evaluation will, one suspects, be based upon the participants' appreciation of how appraisal has assisted the understanding of ministry and stimulated a greater commitment to our discipleship and apostleship. Ultimately, the focus will be and should be felt at the coal face of ministry. If that focus does not bring illumination and warmth it will be the participants, the clergy, who will be the first to inform the systems we devise by either their approbation or rejection. Therein lies the future hope and relevance of the development of appraisal.

References

1   M. Green, *Freed to Serve* (Hodder & Stoughton, London, 1983), ch. 2 and 3.

2   R.W. Southern, *Western Society and the Church in the Middle Ages* (Penguin, Harmondsworth, 1970), ch. 5.

3   M. Jacobs, *Holding in Trust*, New Library of Pastoral Care (SPCK, London, 1989), p. 54.

4   'The role of appraisal in staff development' in L. Bell and C. Day (eds), *Managing the Professional Development of Teachers* (Oxford University, Oxford, 1991), p. 164. Also F. Todd, *Planning Continuing Professional Development* (Croom Helm, Beckenham, 1987), especially sections 'Appraisal of teacher performance' (p. 181) and 'Practice audit model' (p. 27).

5   L. Mead, *Evaluation: of, by, for and to the Clergy* (Alban Institute, Washington, DC, 1990).

6   *The Continuing Education of the Church's Ministry* (GS Misc 122; ACCM, London, 1980).

7   R. Hiscox, J. Gammell and C. Raybould, *Report of the Working Group on Appraisal and Assessment: Ministry Development and Review* (ACCM, London, 1988).

8   *Reports of the National CME Nottingham Conference* (ABM, London, 1992).

3

How to Get the Best out of Appraisal

PETER CRICK

The whole question of ministry appraisal seems to me to revolve around one simple question:

Do I want my work for God to improve?

If the answer to that question is negative then, for a host of reasons, I ought not to be involved in ministry at all! Chief among those reasons would be the lack of vision that could see no need for improvement, or the arrogance that could decide whether anyone's ministry had reached the point of perfection. Either of these stances would render one most unlikely to perform effectively any of the roles usually associated with ministry – viz., pastoral sensitivity, effective communication, prayer, worship, to name but a few.

If the answer is positive, then one has already entered into the realms of 'appraisal' or, better, 'ministry review'. So soon as one desires improvement in ministry the process of review has begun; at least so soon as the question 'How?' has been added to the desire.

As the last chapter showed, there are a variety of patterns of appraisal. In this chapter, whether the purpose of the review is managerial or developmental, the model examined is of consultancy – in which it is assumed that the primary concern is for the minister to develop his or her ministerial potential. Even if the motivating force is managerial, the institutional benefit will still flow through that individual's formation and growth.

Attitudes The effectiveness of any review, however, depends very much upon the attitude with which it is approached, and the methods which are employed. As we are thinking about *ministry* review, it seems self-evident that there must be a theological perception throughout the whole exercise. Even where there appears to be no explicit theology being employed, much is revealed! Take, for example, three responses I have encountered recently:

> Respondent one stated, to the very thought of appraisal, let alone meeting a consultant: 'The Church can require me to live in the place, among the people where I must work. It can even strongly influence *where* I should minister. But I can see no justification at all for it presuming to suggest that I should share anything at all of my ministry with any other colleague. That is just too much!'

Apart from the resentment that trembles within that statement, there is also revealed an individualism – if not isolation – that excludes the wider Church from any part in ministry within that place. The 'Body of Christ' is a truncated doctrine at best in these circumstances. It will be necessary to return to this in more detail later.

> Respondent two stated: 'I have been in touch with my appraisal consultant, and am preparing some material for us to consider together. It's good that I'm finally getting on with it – for I really need a kick up the backside so that I stop dithering around any more!'

Whatever perception of God is held, the Church here certainly has 'authority' with a capital A. While it would seem that the appraisal is being welcomed, there is a low self-image so far as motivation and application are concerned, and it is the outside influence that is going to come in and achieve what past endeavours have failed to do. Or so we hope.

> Respondent three wrote: 'I so valued my time with X. She encouraged me to look at my gifts . . . as used in the parish and in the life of the Church as a whole. This has had the effect of transforming my ministry . . . with an aim and vision . . . shared by clergy and laity . . . this is all very exciting. . . .'

Apart from the tenor of the letter, there is revealed a dimension of relationship between the minister and the Church that is completely absent from the others. It is seen both as an important and valued environment within which ministry is exercised, and also as an enabling body with which he is in direct relationship in all avenues of activity. It is there that his gifts are perceived to have pertinence, direction and life. Consequently, even the vision ceases to be his sole property and thereby grows in stature, being shared by laity and other clergy.

Discipleship It is from the word 'disciple' that we gain the word discipline. Sadly, in much of today's society discipline is seen as a threat and an unwelcome imposition upon our freedom of action and thought. Within the Gospels, however, the disciples are shown to be eager (even if occasionally unable) to soak up every snippet of wisdom and perception that Jesus can impart. And although there are frequent references to the Scriptures and their contents, it is the dynamic interaction with him that shapes the discipline and renders it effective.

It is with such a theological and educational stance that any minister of the Christian faith is most likely to gain maximum benefit. In fact it would seem probable that without such perceptions one would be unlikely to experience much growth or personal development.

The New Testament is scattered with assertions of the need for mutual concern. Jesus says: 'By this shall men know you – that you love one another' and: 'I pray that they may be one as we are one.' After the Ascension, the Christians are described: 'They met constantly to hear the apostles teach, and to share the common life.' Paul teaches radically in the famous passages of Romans, Corinthians and Ephesians about the unity and sharing of responsibility that is necessary, if demonstrably effective Christian ministry is to be seen.

So, having decided that one's ministry needs to improve, it can be argued that the first step that needs to be taken is to look to the wider Church to provide resources to assist the process. The primary resource is personal, and is focused on the person who assists you to discover the discipline your ministry requires as you apply yourself to its review.

Relationships   Relationships are at the heart of our Christian faith. Mention of the Johannine statement 'God is Love' brings a host of other similar expressions and sentiments to mind. Accepting all this as given, it is as well to recognize that at a natural level some relationships establish themselves more immediately and creatively than others. This can need careful attention in a consultative contract. It is not the purview of this chapter to explore the patterns of ministerial review used by the Church. In any case it has already been done elsewhere.[1] Within the entire framework of available options, however, one thing is likely to be crucial. If the review is to be beneficial – to the Church as well as the minister – the review relationship *must* be sound and trusting.

Trust   The concept of appraisal or review is a relatively new one within the Church. Consequently, few people actually seek a ministerial review; most have to be persuaded, or required to engage in the process. When this is the case, it usually means also that the appraiser or reviewer is allocated or suggested to the minister from within a diocesan or regional programme. This carries with it implications that must be faced if real benefit is to accrue either to the minister or the Church in general.

The first requirement of anyone engaging in a review of his or her ministry must be to find someone with whom he or she will feel secure as all the potentially uncomfortable elements of his or her work are exposed. I think this really is essential. Few people are likely to risk disclosure to someone who cannot be relied upon to handle their personal matters sensitively. This is even more likely to be the case if it is an appraisal that is required by higher authority, possibly with a 'line management' involvement. However daunting it may be, it is doubly worth struggling with this issue in such circumstances. (As a wry comment – it is probable that a considerable amount of self- and institutional awareness would develop during such negotiations!)

Of course, 'trust' is a many-faceted jewel in human affairs. For our purposes the following criteria would seem to be the vital ones:

(a) The ability to hold in confidence any private information shared.

(b) A commitment to one's personal well-being within any situation that is met (what Peter Selby describes as 'willingness to walk with me, and fall with me'[2]).

(c) An equal commitment to helping one face that which needs to be faced, however uncomfortable that might be. Love, after all, is a concern for the *best* for the person loved – not simply a constant succession of pats on the head in the midst of all acts of futility. Challenge is sometimes the greatest blessing that can be conferred.

(d) A clarity of perception that is able to identify the nature of issues which require exploration and, just as importantly, an ability to help one exercise the same clarity for oneself and move forward to take action, while owning the decision responsibly.

(e) An acknowledgement that the primary loyalty is to the minister and, through him or her, those to whom he or she ministers. But however important the institutional demands, even in the process of facing them, *this* contract is and must be crucial.

There are, of course, many gifts and skills that a consultant requires to bring full benefit to a reviewee. Volumes have been written, designed to assist them in their task. Our concern here is solely the preparation needed by individuals seeking review. If they have diligently covered the ground outlined in the five points above, they are most unlikely to acquire a consultant lacking many other important abilities.

Objectives   There used to be a succinct little poster that said: 'If you don't know where you're going, you'll end up somewhere else!' Much the same can be said of ministerial review – unless care is taken to think through what it is hoped to achieve in the process, then there is a significant risk of missing some of the opportunities presented.

Most of us involved in Christian ministry have some sense of vocation; of seeking to serve God in his Church, as a result of some sort of 'call' – an impingement upon our lives, believed to be of God, that it was not possible to ignore. Once it has been acknowledged it begins to manifest itself in such ways as:

(a) Preaching the Gospel.
(b) Working with and on behalf of people in Christ's name.
(c) Administering the sacraments.
(d) Enabling the Church more appropriately to be itself whenever it is present.

And so on, according to the individual's perception of the nature of ministry. Sometimes this itself needs to be examined.

Day-to-day-tasks   At the same time, there are specific issues and tasks, with which one can be grappling in a particular place and at a particular time, which also have to be addressed. Sometimes they will be so pressing that they cloud out almost all other concerns in life, let alone ministry. Equally, one might just gently be 'chugging along', delighting in what lies to hand, satisfied that in some way God's people are being served.

Direction It is this broad spectrum of ministry that needs to be reviewed. It is to be brought out for perusal in the presence of a fellow member of Christ's Church. Why? What is it that one hopes will be achieved by this exercise? Is it a re-discovery of faith and sense of vocation? Is it the resolution of a specific problem or dilemma? Is it simply the desire to check out the validity of one's thinking or model of ministry? Whichever of these or any other targets is in mind needs to be identified; for it is the setting of targets that will focus the attention of both the consultant and the minister in their early meetings, and largely determine the direction of their journey together.

Context No one works in a vacuum. There will always be a context for all endeavour. The town, community, district are obvious foci of attention, as is a congregation; but is that congregation to be examined as a recipient or as a source of ministry? Likewise, both congregation and minister are in relation to other parts of the Church and society. These sometimes ambivalent corporate relationships frequently play a major role in influencing the state of play in individuals and smaller units. 'They' are a well-known enemy of all pure effort-where-it-matters workers, or a drain upon resources; or even, once in a while, a reservoir of inspiration and loyalty. It is as well to spend some time taking a realistic look at all of this, and assessing how one wishes to respond ministerially in the future.

Interpersonal skills Ministry is almost entirely about people. Even administration has as its ultimate objective the facilitating of human interaction. Tracking one's way through the labyrinths of a community's inter- and intra-relationships requires many skills and much sensitivity. This is doubly true if 'Kingdom events' are to be the outcome of the endeavour. Much ministerial frustration is the result of insufficient knowledge in this area of activity. The behavioural sciences are a natural bedfellow of pastoral theology, and it is a lonely ministerial bed from which either is absent.

Preparation All of this needs to be explored carefully in private, before any meeting with the consultant. The responses to it will inform the voice as well as the words. Re-examined episodes will expose subliminal motives and emotions that can often be found to control all manner of seemingly innocuous behaviour.

When this has been done as thoroughly as possible, it is necessary to sift it. A good consultant is usually going to want some information before the review session. Unless one has been excessively inactive, it is most unlikely to be possible to put even a digest of all the subject matter we have intimated above in a manageable form. Thus, it will be necessary to select the subjects, activities and issues that seem most important, and present them in a digestible form. This at least informs the reviewer of some basic ground that is to be covered. Even the reasons for the selected priorities having that level of importance can be informative to a sensitive examination. A frequent surprise is the discovery of the significance of something previously unrecognized!

The need for change One final piece of self-preparation is necessary. What we have been describing here is the examination of the full spectrum of activity of someone who is involved in part of the work of God, within the organization that we believe to be the present Body of Christ here on earth. This is the same God who said, according to John, 'Behold I make all things new'.[3] So if this review is conducted consciously as a godly event, it is as well to be prepared – even desirous – that things will change in the future. One might even discover change in oneself!

> To seek to find one's self is to risk getting lost or, far worse, becoming lost. The risk is patent but there is no alternative to risks other than stagnation.[4]

The appraisal   It is not now appropriate to delve into the actual encounter with the consultant.

Decisions   As will be shown elsewhere (in Chapter 5), however, it is more than probable that the minister will be helped to come to a point of understanding that leads to a decision to act. It might be some small action, or something major; that doesn't concern us here. What does concern us is the use made of that decision. Firstly, and most importantly, it must be the minister's own decision. It is no use at all setting about a course of action on which, deep in the heart, there are doubts. If it goes wrong it would then be so easy to disown one's proper share of responsibility. Part of this process of evolving the decision or plan would probably include a careful questioning by both the minister and the consultant, which would involve the pruning of all action for which the reasons were uncertain. This is also likely to include a serious attempt to judge the possible results of any action or decision.

Change   The questioning process itself is as valuable as any decisions made. The reasons that might lurk behind original motives and these final decisions can be amazingly revealing. Carefully explored alongside one's working context, perceptions of role and objectives, it is possible to reach levels of understanding of one's whole self and potential that can be life-changing, disconcerting and exciting beyond any previous expectation.

Whether the action is to be a relatively passive, private matter (like regularizing times of rest, for example), or something highly active and public (like some confrontation or structural change), a plan and a timetable should be agreed with the consultant. This should include further review.

Application By the time the minister and the consultant have parted, it is evident that a considerable amount of time and effort will have been expended. All of this will have been directed at the situation in which the minister works, and the way in which that ministry is conducted. If all this is not to be wasted – or at least under-utilized – it is important that the minister sets about diligently, and in a disciplined manner, implementing any lessons learned or plans formulated.

If the consultant has been chosen wisely, then the action plan will conform to the following criteria:

> Action should have built-in standards by which to measure progress and results; lead to further data collection and change, if evaluation shows it to be going in the wrong direction relative to the chosen goals; be continuously based on research, once the process has begun.[5]

It should also include a detailed awareness of the other members of the congregation or community within which the minister works.

That said, much recommends the 'KISS' principle of Robert Gallagher – 'Keep It Simple, Stupid'![6] The problem with human interaction is that it can be so complex. · One action can have implications in a multitude of places and among a wide sector of any community. If several initiatives are implemented at once it can be difficult to determine what has caused what to happen. So easily observed, one-step actions are simpler to monitor and evaluate, and more satisfying when identifiable results are seen to occur.

The journal   One of the best habits that any 'people-worker' can develop is the keeping of a journal, and the period after a ministry review is probably the best and easiest time to begin. Not many of us have the diligence of Pepys or that Edwardian Lady, so keeping a day-by-day chronicle of all we experience is too much to ask. In any case, unless we have extraordinary luck we would be unlikely to be published! But to keep a journal is an altogether different exercise.

What is involved is simple. Whenever one takes a significant step, or engages in a noteworthy encounter, or has a thought or experience that affects one's working activity, relationships or attitudes, it is noted down in the journal. Likewise, when anything happens as a result of observed behaviour or one's own initiatives, note it down and mark the co-relationship if it is obvious. Sometimes it is possible to go for weeks and write nothing. At other times an entry will need to be made almost daily for a prolonged period. It does not usually take very long, however, for discernible patterns of cause and effect, change of attitude or shift of emphasis to begin to be clear. This is generally more evident if one does not read back over past entries too frequently, so that patterns have time to reveal themselves, rather than being forced into the text.

Such a record is invaluable. It is particularly helpful and supportive for the minister between reviews, as he or she seeks to develop the work progressively. It is also an incisive tool when studied in company with a trusted consultant who participated in the thinking which led to the actions and responses that now unfold.

So far our minister has taken two steps as a result of engaging in the appraisal exercise:

- He or she has implemented a plan that was carefully thought out and analysed by him- or herself, under the scrutiny of the consultant.
- A journal has been kept that allows an adequate supervision of the progress of that plan.

One further thing is necessary, which has been implicit in much of the text that has gone before. Further review is crucial. The original disquiet, or desire for improvement, that started the review process will almost certainly have been intensified by all that has gone on thus far. It would be almost impossible to assess it all adequately from within, without the different perspective of an outside observer's critique.

Evaluation

> Brief and cursory reflection upon deep and extended experience is not likely to yield up much truth-value; similarly with elaborate and prolonged reflection upon a fleeting trace of experience.[7]

This was said about a different pattern of working, namely group co-counselling. But its truth applies equally to our concern here – how a minister who has decided to review his or her ministry using a consultant can get the best out of the whole exercise.

If the review has been a traumatic, soul-searching appraisal of the whole of the individual's vocation and direction in life, with consequent major upheaval and change of direction, then a prolonged period of deliberation will be unavoidable. If it has been a more limited exercise, possibly only being a consideration of achievements to date, and thought about further options, then a shorter period of time would suffice. It is nonetheless advisable to pursue some evaluative reflection:

> Only learners themselves can learn, and only they can reflect on their own experiences.[8]

Criteria There are some definite pointers that can help evaluation:

1 The relationship with the consultant should have enhanced the ability to recognize and accept *feelings*; and to better

perceive the part they play in the exercise of ministry. It is likely, for instance, that strong feelings will have accompanied the process of ministry review. Exploring these will probably lead into an examination of the emotions that accompany and influence everyday activity.

2 There should be a greater ability to recognize the quality and nature of relationships within the community where the minister works; and an ability to better integrate and accept the contribution of others in full acknowledgement of their individuality and worth.

3 There should be a clearer understanding of the nature of the role that needs to be fulfilled by the minister in his or her particular place, and the expectations which accompany it.

4 No one can be omnicompetent. But there should be a better awareness of the principal skills needed at this time; the primary ability to differentiate between fact and mere impression.

5 The individual sense of personal worth should increase, such that attention to the self can be accepted as a good thing – without guilt or embarrassment – that is necessary to nurture the strength and emotional stability required for a demanding office and responsibility.

Assessment   There are two areas of perception and experience, however, which represent *the* litmus test.

Theology   It is *Christian* ministry that is our concern. Ministers need to ascertain whether appraisal has helped to develop their faith and vocation. Has their perception of their role and the people among whom they work been changed in a godly manner? The understanding of personal commitment should be clearer. The direction in which life and ministry could develop should be able to be seen as opportunity rather than hazard. Even the possibility of failure can become a theological reality that includes ˙ the concept of resurrection, progression and acceptance.

Change of direction can be discovered still to be in the presence of God.

In short, it is the affirmation of the self, in the midst of so complex and potentially confusing a web of relationships and issues, that is the primary function of the consultant. In both an emotional and a spiritual sense it can represent salvation.

Ecclesiology A similar criterion applies to the apprehension of the Church. All ministry is exercised in the name of, and by, the Church. Too frequently this truth is contradicted by our disordered perceptions, which lead us to behave as if our work were our exclusive possession. Yet if there is any spiritual truth in the doctrine that we are the Body of Christ here on earth, then surely the process of our interaction as Christians should develop the quality of our *corporate* relationship with God, whom Jesus came to reveal to us? In fact it can be argued that it is only by this means that God can be made tangible – incarnate – in the present day. If there is any validity in this perception, then review/appraisal should enhance the minister's comprehension of the reality of God in his or her own life, through the consultant's ministry as an explicit representative of the wider Church.

Likewise, there should be noticeable, creative change in the minister's awareness of the people among whom his or her ministry is being performed. There should in time be greater unity and mutual perception, and realization of ministers' local need for each other's gifts, if the Christian Gospel is to be adequately proclaimed in their place. It is after all the *Church*'s ministry, that is being exercised. The more this becomes recognized, inevitably the more extensive will become the involvement of the wider Church.

Telos and charisma If this even begins to occur, then the minister concerned can consider the review not only successful, but a gift of God from the people of God.

References

1   M. Jacobs, *Holding in Trust* (SPCK, London, 1989). R. Hiscox, J. Gammell and C. Raybould, *Report of the Working Group on Appraisal and Assessment* (ACCM, London, 1988).

2   P. Selby, *Liberating God* (SPCK, London,1983).

3   Revelation 21.5.

4   A. Blumberg and R.T. Golembiewski, *Learning and Change in Groups* (Penguin, Harmondsworth, 1976), p. 144.

5   G. Lippitt and R. Lippitt, *The Consulting Process in Action* (University Associates Press, La Jolla, California, 1978), p. 85.

6   R. Gallagher, *Action Plans – Consultation Skills Working Manual* (Mid Atlantic Training Assoc., 1979).

7   J. Heron in *Reflection: Turning Experience into Learning* (see note 8), p. 131.

8   D. Boud, R. Keogh and D. Walker (eds), *Reflection: Turning Experience Into Learning* (Kogan Page, London, 1985), p. 11.

4

Appraisal and Accountability

GEOFFREY BABB

The question of accountability The independence of the Anglican clergy has been greatly prized in the past and is still defended in the present. With the freehold, it is said, the parish priest is able to withstand inappropriate pressure from bishop or congregation if their expectations are not met. The disapproval of neighbouring fellow clergy can be disregarded from behind the defences of the parish boundaries. Such security of tenure, together with the lack of formal accountability implicit in these arrangements, makes the clergy unique among the professions. Abuses of the freehold have sometimes been notorious, but the greater danger has surely been that it has not required the minister to work at building mutually supportive and collaborative relationships with lay people. Commenting on the value attributed to the freehold, the Morley Report said:

> As well as being a bastion for the prophet and sturdy reformer, or a support to the timid, the freehold has on occasions served as a wall to protect the lazy and the indifferent, and as a means of perpetuating a ministry which is not for the good of the Church.
>
> (*Partners in Ministry*, 1967, p. 50)

In the 1960s the Morley Report and its predecessor, the Paul Report, argued for changes in the system of patronage and the clergy freehold and proposed new ways of deploying the parish clergy. Successive measures enacted since then have resulted in a variety of patterns for the provision of ministry in the parishes and some weakening of the freehold system. In spite of this the freehold has remained, and the independence it confers on the clergy is still largely intact. Perhaps especially, the idea lingers on that the preservation of the freehold is essential to the integrity of parish ministry.

Changing patterns of ministry It is easy to forget just how much has changed in relation to ordained ministry over the past generation or so. The payment of the clergy has been centralized and they have become (for purposes of National Insurance) employees rather than self-employed. Glebe and endowments which provided a local income for each benefice have been transferred to the centre. A particular focus of change, at the beginning of the 1990s, is the need for an increasing proportion of the cost of the remuneration of the clergy to be found at the local level, by the parishes themselves. There are signs that lay people, bearing this greater cost, will demand greater accountability from their clergy.

A likely, and desirable, consequence of this development is that the Church might begin to pay greater attention than hitherto to the professional development of its paid clergy and to demand that they are properly equipped for their ministry. However, the Free Churches and the Roman Catholic Church have for a long time depended on congregational giving for the maintenance of the ordained ministry. It might be instructive to explore what has been learned there, especially as these Churches offer contrasting models of the centralization or dispersal of authority.

Team ministries were intended to offer a different pattern from that of the sole incumbent, in which collegiality and accountability, at least within the clergy team, are expected and valued. Yet financial pressures, again, are prompting a more urgent reorganization. The suspension of presentation to benefices when they fall vacant means that more clergy are likely to be appointed as priests-in-charge than in the past. The greater the burden of pastoral ministry on the remaining parish clergy the greater becomes the need to harness the gifts of lay people to share the pastoral task. There are more non-stipendiary ministers, some of whom take on responsibility for churches and their congregations, and with whom stipendiary clergy have to collaborate. The number of specialist and sector ministers has increased; unlike parish clergy they tend to have fixed contracts and clear lines of accountability to those who oversee their work.

An unhelpful model Changes such as these represent significant moves away from the received pattern of the minister's independence. However, the freehold persists and so does the model of clerical independence which it represents. This means that it still exerts a powerful influence on the understanding which both clergy and congregations have of the status, authority and autonomy of the clergy within the parish. In many parishes it makes little difference whether the minister is beneficed or not; in practice there is likely to be no more accountability required from day to day of a priest-in-charge than of a beneficed incumbent.

There are several ways in which the received model is unhelpful, both for the clergy and for the Church as a whole. The privileged position of the clergy can be an obstacle to the development of lay initiative and responsibility in the life of the Church. It still easily happens that:

> the clergy to no small extent dictate the forms and boundaries of lay responsibility, activity, spirituality and learning.
> (*All Are Called*, 1985, p. 16)

Lay people are more likely now to expect a different, more open attitude to them, their lives in the world and their part in the Church's life. For them, the minister no longer carries an authority which cannot be questioned.

The need to preserve independence of action may be used

by the minister to justify isolating him- or herself, and the congregation too, from fresh currents of thinking and practice which may be flowing in the wider Church. In the same way, the minister may use this as an excuse for avoiding the responsibility to pay proper attention to professional needs and development, whether that is in relation to the demands of current responsibilities or in preparing for the possible future development of his or her ministry.

Working alone in a parish may require a wide range of skills which cannot possibly be expected of one person. The lone incumbent may thus struggle with some aspects of work for which inclination, talent or both are lacking. Yet the prevailing assumption is that the minister is, or should be, competent in all areas of ministry. Such an ethos discourages the minister from seeking advice, support or training from outside the situation and from looking to members of the congregation to share some of the burdens and tasks which come with parish ministry.

In these and other ways the ministry of the clergy may be weakened and their energy easily dissipated. Having completed over fifty appraisals with his clergy, a bishop found that one thing becoming clear to him was that perhaps as many as half of the clergy are falling short in their ministry. By that he did not only mean that some clergy fail to carry out their work adequately. He could also see that far more fail to realize the potential which they possess for effective ministry and which was presumably recognized and encouraged at the outset. Many factors have been summoned up to explain the supposed problems and failings of the clergy, but it is hard to avoid the conclusion that the isolation and unaccountability that go with our present ordering of parish ministry are a major reason for this.

Patterns of work   The pattern of work in parish ministry is not easily planned and managed. Plans for how a day or week is to be spent can be disrupted by the need to respond to immediate problems: a pastoral crisis or a funeral will prevent attendance at a meeting; time for prayer, reflection and study may be swallowed up by other, more insistent, pressures. The shaping of a vision for the parish and long-term planning can be lost in the need to tackle short-term problems. Divisions in the congregation can sap the minister's energy and prevent movement forward. There is always a balancing act, which requires an acute awareness to the changing context, between ministry to the congregation and ministry which is shared with them, between standing apart from the congregation and identifying with them. When the minister looks beyond the local situation, it may be difficult to see how the work which she or he is doing in the parish fits into the direction being taken by the diocese or by the wider Church.

The difficulties are compounded by the frequent failure to find someone with the skills to act as a sounding board or consultant to the minister, in spite of the existence of schemes for work consultancy in many dioceses. Time and again I am struck by how glad clergy are, once they have decided or been persuaded to take the time to stand back from their work, to have the opportunity to review their ministry in a safe and supportive environment, to share their experiences and to work their way through some of the issues which face them in the parish. Time and space for this reflection with an alert and supportive listener needs to be a regular part of any minister's working life.

Creating accountability   If accountability is not built into the structures within which we work as ministers, then it may be important, for ourselves and others, to say nothing of the work we are doing, to create our own framework for giving account of ourselves. This will mean that within our working relationships with other people, individuals or groups, we are prepared to be open in our own activities and honest in our reporting of them, and to be responsive to what we hear from other people. We hope for mutuality and collaboration in any shared enterprise, but especially within the Church as the Body of Christ, united in fellowship and in commitment to the Church's task.

If it is a basic problem that:

> our Church's structures have not yet found good ways of taking many of its clergy and laity into an effective partnership for learning the will of God for our day
>
> (*All Are Called*, 1985, p. 10)

then we have to search for those ways ourselves at the local level. Collaboration between people and accountability to one another go hand in hand, however informally this is expressed. We may have to become more open and more vulnerable in order to become better at collaborative ministry.

Yet it is easy for these matters to slip from our grasp. It is possible for an incumbent to have correct and formal dealings with churchwardens and other lay officers; it is also possible to be thoroughly friendly with them. In either case, the incumbent can entirely fail to acknowledge any accountability to them. Similarly, the PCC is there to be consulted on some matters; on others it has decisions to make for itself. Again, it is perfectly possible to do everything according to what is required and laid down, but never enter into a truly collaborative relationship with the PCC and never give any hint of being accountable to it and open to its perceptions of the common task.

Most of us can give instances of the creative consequences of making our own work available for the scrutiny of others. When I began to work as a diocese's first social responsibility officer, I was largely left to my own devices. After some years of developing our work from small beginnings it was decided that the Board for Social Responsibility should have a standing committee to help the Board as a whole cope with the increasing number of issues coming before it. In that small group my work as executive officer was subjected to greater scrutiny and I increasingly carried out work which had been discussed and agreed upon by this group, rather than simply chosen by myself or, at best, discussed between the Board's (episcopal) chairman and myself. The new arrangement not only resulted in a more effective and collaborative process for the Board's work, but also gave me more support as I went about my role on the Board's behalf. It is this sense of collaboration and being supported in the work we do which (for a variety of reasons) is so frequently lacking in the Church and amongst its ordained ministers. Yet opportunities abound in the parish for entering into formal or informal groups in which it is possible to create this way of working.

Understanding appraisal Appraisal is clearly one way in which we put our work before other people in order that we might become clearer about what is going on in it and what issues are at stake. It is a means by which we can come to an overview of our ministry, the direction it is taking and the matters which we need to address in order to become more effective as ministers. It enables us to put our goals and our work within the context of the institution's goals and the other work being done within it and on its behalf.

An appraisal within a formally arranged system usually results in an agreed report which becomes part of the individual's record of ministry held by the bishop. In that, it differs from a work consultation, which reviews the current sphere of work and the issues which are being faced within it, and then determines goals to pursue within it. The outcome of this process is for the minister alone to pursue. Both appraisal and consultation are quite different from spiritual direction, which focuses on the person in relation to God, though it is inevitable that matters of ministry and spirituality are closely interwoven in the life of the minister.

The introduction of a scheme for the appraisal of ministry holds out both a threat and a promise to the clergy who are expected or invited to participate. The threat may lie in the assumption that appraisal involves the assessment and judgement of a person's ministry. Another threat may lie in the minister's fear that the particular circumstances which she or he faces will not be understood, or that judgements will be made and recorded which will adversely affect the direction of her or his future ministry. The minister's sense of independence and authority within the parish may be undermined if the appraisal process seems to be calling her or his ministry into question. If the diocesan hierarchy is directly involved in carrying out appraisals, it may be difficult to relate the degree of closeness which the appraisal interview requires to the distance which is normally part of the minister's relationship with the bishop or archdeacon.

Effectiveness in ministry   In any case, it may be asked, how can any conclusions be reached about something as intangible as ministry? Is effectiveness in ministry going to be understood simply in terms of a thriving and growing congregation and financial stability? Are there no hard questions to ask of a successful minister and congregation? How will a ministry which seems to be marked by struggle and failure be received? In reflecting on our own or anyone else's ministry there is a powerful theological justification for looking beyond the servicing of the institution and the settled congregation. There is also a wealth of theological sources to guide our reflections on these matters, including a great deal in the Gospels about weakness, vulnerability and failure.

Maybe anything which puts the spotlight upon us and our work, and which might bring into the open what we would prefer to keep hidden even from ourselves, is bound to be perceived as threatening. Certainly other professions have also felt the tension between what is offered by appraisal and the hidden dangers and threats, as well as the worry about whose purpose is being served by the process – the organization's or the individual's. Discussing the pros and cons of appraisal and evaluation, Mary Anne Coate concludes:

> The lack of evaluation may apparently protect the more vulnerable aspects of our self-esteem, but the potential for

developing self-esteem through a sensitive and supportive evaluation process is also lost.

(Coate, 1989, p. 142)

The promise which is held out by appraisal lies in being taken notice of and listened to, in having the issues which, arise in your work understood, your work acknowledged in a wider context, and the development of your ministerial career taken seriously. When this promise is fulfilled by what actually happens in the appraisal, then there is a real sense of being supported in your ministry. This does not mean that no hard questions are to be asked or that awkward matters are to be avoided. Stewart Cross, the former Bishop of Blackburn, had earlier worked for many years in the BBC. He said that he experienced more pastoral support through his annual and very rigorous career appraisal by his superiors in the BBC than he ever experienced in the Church. We are, in fact, only just past the beginning of discovering what is offered by appraisal of ministry.

Telling other people what we are doing and what is going on for us, telling the story of our life and giving account of ourselves all form part of the continuing conversation we have with other people throughout our life. Such conversation is informal and unstructured; it does not necessarily fit into any larger and more purposeful pattern. However, the telling of our story is the first step towards analysis and reflection; it simply needs a framework and a purposiveness about it to become a tool for constructive reflection on our work and activity. At its most basic level a scheme for work appraisal is the formalizing of a structure within which people can give an account of themselves so that it helps both the individual and the organization towards a greater clarity about the enterprise as a whole and the individual's role within it.

Appraisal and accountability　A number of surveys have been made of the appraisal schemes operated by the dioceses of the Church of England (e.g. Hiscox *et al.*, 1988; Seed, 1992). A recent report prepared for the Advisory Board of Ministry in 1992 found that within the great diversity of diocesan schemes there was also a confusing diversity of stated objectives for these schemes. A list of stated aims of diocesan schemes included the following:

> being pastoral and supportive,
> providing an opportunity for reflection and review on a person's ministry,
> identifying training needs and establishing directions for future training,
> assisting the bishop in making appointments.
> (*Report on CME Officers' Regional Meetings*, 1992)

It is apparent from such aims that appraisal is not intended by the dioceses to be a way of managing the work of the clergy or a tool for exerting control or discipline over them. However, the diversity of schemes, and even more, the diversity of understandings of appraisal, have the potential for diminishing the usefulness of appraisal for the Church as a whole.

There is a need to build up, across the dioceses with their different schemes, an understanding of the purpose of appraisal and what constitutes good practice. The issue of the diversity of schemes has to be tackled, and especially the division between those in which appraisal is carried out by someone in the diocesan hierarchy and those which involve self-appraisal (with or without a consultant to help). From the point of view of encouraging a greater sense of accountability to the wider Church and not simply to themselves and their work, the former may well be preferable, and have in fact been adopted by the majority of dioceses.

What is needed, too, is for appraisals to be conducted with sufficient consistency, fairness and openness about their purpose and their outcome that the fears which are so easily aroused in the clergy are gradually dispelled. The relationship of appraisal to other resources for helping clergy tackle issues in their ministry (work consultancy, spiritual direction or whatever) needs to be clearly stated. The appraisal process must be handled in such a way that it is effective, and perceived to be effective, in helping individual clergy with their ministry and in helping towards the gradual improvement of the understanding and skills to be found among the clergy as a body.

Real, but manageable, proposals emerging from the appraisal for future action by the individual can cover the current sphere of work, the development of ministerial gifts and understanding, specific directions for participation in ongoing training, and the minister's personal well-being. These proposals should be supported through the availability of the resources to ensure that they are followed up.

We have argued that the long-standing issue of the accountability of the clergy has been sharpened by the growing emphasis on collaborative ministry and by the changing expectations of lay people. Appraisal offers a way of promoting accountability simply because it asks the minister to give an account of her or his ministry. It is also important that within the appraisal process questions are raised about collaboration and accountability. This means giving careful attention to the relationships and groups which are significant in the day-to-day work of the minister. How easy does the minister find it to submit her or his work to the scrutiny of Church members and to share reflection, decision-making and action with them? Does the minister's leadership allow other people to develop their own skills in leadership and exercise power and authority for themselves alongside the clergy? In this way appraisal can help with the task of opening up the life of the Church (and not only in the parishes) to the possibilities of collaboration. This in turn would have profound and far-reaching consequences for the effectiveness of all our efforts to live and proclaim the Gospel.

References

All Are Called: Towards a Theology of the Laity (CIO, London, 1985).

Mary Anne Coate, *Clergy Stress* (SPCK, London, 1989).

R. Hiscox, J. Gammell and C. Raybould, *Report of the Working Group on Appraisal and Assessment*, made to the CME Committee of ACCM (ACCM, London, 1988).

Partners in Ministry (CIO, London, 1967).

Leslie Paul, *The Deployment and Payment of the Clergy* (CIO, London, 1964).

Report on CME Officers' Regional Meetings, made to the Ministry Development and Deployment Committee of ABM (1992).

R. Seed, 'Clergy appraisal in the Church of England', *Crucible* (October 1992).

5

The Perception of the Clergy

RICHARD SEED

An anonymous article, under the pseudonym of 'Flabellum', in the *Church Observer* during 1990 shows in an extreme and yet rather helpful way the fear of mentioning the possibility of appraisal to clergy within the Church of England:

> The Archbishop of Canterbury has announced his approval of 'Clergy Appraisal'. Not just for hack Parish Priests like 'Flabellum' but even for Bishops! I volunteer my services to assess the 'performance' of all Diocesan Bishops. This will be a time-consuming task – as I have already spent many fruitless hours in training the present episcopate of the Church of England! One Bishop admitted to me after his first six months in the job, that, had he realised it meant dealing with so many clergy problems, he doubted he would have accepted. No doubt this explains why he is still a suffragan Bishop!
>
> How should we assess the performance of a Parish Priest? Numbers of people in the pews? T.V. appearances or sex appeal? His amount of influence within a local community on local issues? His political leanings? The quality of his university degree? How many hours he spends daily in prayer? Does he say the Rosary?
>
> Where we start on assessment surely gives more information about the assessors, than about those to be assessed.
>
> What is to be done about the information gained? Priests

can be sacked – but only after long and cumbersome procedures which aren't really Christian. A Priest can be
re-trained to put right alleged deficiencies but what about the
Prophet in a parish that rejects prophecy?

Our Archbishop seems keen on managerial structures.
But would such structures have allowed the 12 Apostles to
have functioned as leaders of Christ's Church? With no education, great impetuosity, simple life-style – they wouldn't
have lasted five minutes in a 'Corporate plan' Church. Many
priests and laity feel that in recent years ACCM have laid
too much emphasis on candidates for the Priesthood being
academically and socially 'right'. This attitude has been
reinforced for many in the closing of most establishments
that trained Priests from ordinary working-class back-
grounds. The Curé d'Ars had great difficulty in getting himself ordained because he wasn't very intellectual or socially
acceptable. Today, he is the Patron Saint of Parish Priests.
Our urge to copy the management procedures of the secular
world may in the end mean that we have a Priesthood which
is not attuned to the mind of Christ.

(Flabellum, 1990)

However, this article is helpful in its extremism, if only to
show the depth of fear and misunderstanding that the word
'appraisal' has caused. To many, appraisal is seen as the
world of industry and commerce invading the ranks of
the ministry. It embraces many other terms which describe
the examination or reflection of ministry. This process can
be undertaken either hierarchically or mutually with other
clergy or alone with an external consultant. Either way,
various names such as assessment, audit, consultancy,
discussion, evaluation, review, supervision, support, can all
be used to mean the same thing: namely, the removal of
clergy unaccountability and isolation in order that instead
there can be a mutual awareness of ministry and its development. Canon Ian Hardaker, the Clergy Appointments
Adviser, in a paper circulated to diocesan bishops, strongly
supports a 'structured system of appraisal' of the work of
the clergy. He sees the need for such a system as a result of

his experience in dealing with many clergy seeking appointments through his central network. The need is great, he says, not only to enhance clergy performance but also to act as an antidote to loneliness. Hardaker states:

> I am concerned by the number of men and women whom I see and with whom I discuss their present work and their style of ministry who express an appreciation of the questions I ask and the interest I show. Many say that this is the first time anyone has ever shown that degree of interest in them and their work. Further, the style and content of references written by Bishops in response to requests from me suggests that in some instances Bishops do not have any detailed information about the style of a man or woman's ministry, their strengths and weaknesses. In a number of cases further investigation suggests that it is not just lack of information but even wrong information which lies behind a reference. This is of particular concern as a man's prospects may be put in jeopardy, not just for advancement but for any paid full time ministry.
>
> (Hardaker, 1990)

Hardaker believes that the primary purpose of appraisal is not to be seen as promotion potential but rather the pastoral concern for the minister and his work. It is, therefore, an extension of the traditional care of clergy by the bishop being exercised in a *structured and regular manner*. Appraisal can offer the opportunities for shared reflection and mutual discussion which are so valuable in a situation where the expectation of the individual public role exceeds realism. Talking in detail about one's ministry is an encouragement to overcome an often self-imposed isolation. Ministry, in the Church of England, is often exercised alone, and if appraisal begins to alleviate that isolation and challenge the remoteness of the centre or 'establishment', then it is to be welcomed in order that all can begin to relate to each other as befits a shared ministry in the common life of the Body of Christ.

Why is appraisal necessary? This is a complex question, but those seeking to introduce appraisal schemes need to be able to answer it if any such scheme is to be taken seriously by those expected to take part. There needs to be honesty in answering this question, so reassuring the appraised that there is no hidden, sinister agenda. Much will hang upon the introduction of a scheme and the explanation of its necessity.

The clergy have often been seen as a profession, in the way that recruitment and training are carried out as well as in the local exercise of their work. However, the clergy have a responsibility within the Church, which as a community has a particular message to proclaim, of the Gospel and the Kingdom of God. 'The minister is called to be a sign to the whole Church and to the world of the common vocation to ministry, and as such to be a representative figure' (ACCM, 1980, p. 9).

If professional clergy are understood not as people of a certain status but rather as having a representative activity within a community, then that begins to clarify not only their role but also their accountability to the institution that they represent. Clergy should not be isolated people doing a job totally alone. They represent the community of the Church, not just as a private ego trip but as a call by God through the Church to represent and serve it, a call often described as a 'vocation'.

As a vocation, it is easy to highlight the differences between a job which is unaccountable and one which has representative status and should therefore possess some degree of accountability to the institution it represents. 'Vocation' can too easily be a blurred general term which means different things to different people.

It is, however, within that interaction between the person, the message and the represented community that appraisal is being encouraged as a method of developing a more effective and professional ministry:

> Ministry is an activity of the whole Church, clergy and laity

together. Within that ministry accredited ministers have particular roles. Clearly they have a responsibility for teaching and caring for the people of God, but also they become the focus for certain expectations on the part of society. They are seen as public representatives of the Church and may be recognisable as 'access points' at which members of the community at large may encounter the Church and the Gospel. They are professionals and comparable with members of other professions. The word 'profession' and even more 'professional' is not one that is easily or happily used in the Church. We use it here not in any way to ascribe status but to describe a distinctive style of activity. The life of a professional is chiefly characterised by the way in which the person himself and the institution he represents interact. As medicine is often discovered through an encounter with a doctor, or the law through an encounter with a lawyer or a policeman, so too the minister embodies the institution he represents. He invests himself personally in his work. For many the Church and the Gospel are what he is. Whatever his personal ability or attractiveness, these cannot release him from taking public responsibility for the Church. Equally his public role will not wholly obscure any personal deficiencies he may have. If, therefore, he is to work effectively the minister will need to understand himself within this context, appreciating as far as he may both the various expectations which are held of him and how he is responding to them.

(ACCM, 1980, p. 9)

A priest of the Church of England is ordained into a role which expects him to preach and pastorally minister to his congregation as well as to the wider society of the parish. When instituted to the incumbency of a parish he receives from the bishop the reminder that ministry is a joint 'cure of souls'. In the Church, as the Body of Christ, ministry is to be seen not in isolation but as co-operation with each other. Isolation is discouraged in order that, by reviewing the work of ministry with someone who shares the same task, a person can be enabled to develop greater ministerial skills and so strengthen the witness of the ministry of the Church.

What is its purpose?   Appraisal and spiritual direction are not the same thing and it is important that they remain totally separate. The latter may actually demand more skill and confidentiality than the former. There is at the moment a great dearth of spiritual directors in the Church of England, which may explain why there is such a demand for appraisal. It is, however, not just in order to reflect on life and ministry that appraisal may be necessary.

In most organizations the human resources are the greatest asset. In the Church, not only are the co-operation and involvement of the laity essential but the morale of the clergy is a vital contribution to the total mission in which the Church is engaged:

> One often hears the word 'morale' applied to the feeling which exudes from an apparently satisfied staff of an organisation. Morale is one of those concepts, like 'beauty' or 'freedom', which can be observed when it is present and noticed when it is absent – but precise definition is difficult.
> (Randell, 1972, p. 14)

Morale may be difficult to define, but it is closely linked with motivation, which is best achieved when people feel encouraged to participate in determining their objectives and in the management of their affairs. Appraisal is one aspect of enabling the individual to participate effectively in the development of his job. Dr Edgar Anstey lists five important objectives of effective participation:

1) That people are aware of the aims of the organisation and how their own jobs are contributing to organisational objectives.
2) That people know what is expected of them in their job, and have as much say as possible in how they carry out their work.

70

3) That people are involved in decisions which they perceive as affecting them.
4) That there is a good match between people's skills and abilities and the jobs they have to do, and careers available to them. This has implications for job content as well as recruitment and allocation.
5) That jobs are defined in terms of what was to be achieved rather than the process by which this is done and that recognition is on the basis of this.

(Anstey, 1976, p. 17)

Appraisal is therefore a tool for developing an effective participation by the members of an organization in its aims and objectives. It will also identify what resources are needed to encourage such involvement and, if it is effective, is bound to affect the relationship between all the members of an organization. Some will oppose the introduction of clergy appraisal as another dimension of business management which is out of place in the Church. Others will welcome it as a means of improving and encouraging ministry and thereby enabling it to be more effective.

In 1981, at St George's House, Windsor, a workshop defined clergy appraisal as valuable in the following three areas:

1) for a priest's own discipline through which he can reflect on his own ministry and assess it.
2) to help solve some difficulties over appointments by providing reliable knowledge about a man's ministry.
3) to assess the ministry of the whole church in an area and therefore the combined ministry of priest and people.

(Hiscox, 1988, p. 2)

Appraisal can sound a very daunting new prospect, and considerable emphasis needs to be placed not only upon the manner of its introduction but also upon the attention that it receives and the seriousness with which it is regarded. Industry and commerce now have regular appraisal schemes

71

for all staff. Loren Mead, for the Alban Institute in Washington, sees four areas that are invaluable in the evaluation of any person's work as:

1) the person
2) the task to be done
3) the way the task is performed by the person
4) the context within which the task is done.

(Mead, 1990, p. 2)

Who will do it? In many dioceses ministry review is conducted by the bishop or archdeacon, whilst they in turn are reviewed by some other line management outside the diocese. The dioceses that do not use the 'senior staff' prefer the scheme to be of a 'self-appraisal' method where the individual may choose from a list of people available.

The diocese of Durham, for example, has three particular levels of operation: (a) self-appraisal; (b) consultancy; (c) action. It is a diocese which has a strong theological use of the Ordinal and encourages those clergy who trust each other to reflect upon a series of pre-arranged questions arising from the implications of the Ordinal. Every ordained person in the diocese, including all senior staff and the bishops, is committed to this practice of self-appraisal and reflection.

Several dioceses encourage a scheme of self-appraisal which is usually based on the use of external consultants who are prepared to discuss with clergy their work and help them to evaluate their ministry. Interestingly, in these schemes the initiative rests with the individual clergy to make the first approach. The diocese of Gloucester, however, encourages the particular consultant to contact the clergy, which could be commendable if he or she is showing a genuine interest. It would be negative if the impression was given of an overbearing, somewhat heavy approach, but at least it reminds the clergy that such a scheme exists!

There seems much to commend those schemes where there is some involvement with the local bishop. The Church of England, as an episcopal church, sees ministry essentially and theologically as a co-operative exercise between the bishop and the clergy. The words used at the institution of a new incumbent emphasize that the new ministry beginning is a mutual sharing: 'Receive the Cure of Souls, which is both yours and mine.'

The role of the bishop in ministerial review should be an aspect of his care for and interest in the clergy of the diocese. There are, of course, some obvious drawbacks! Some well-meaning bishops may be so zealous in their schemes that they could appear somewhat high-handed, and the appraisal would merely follow their own expectation of ministry, which could be rather limited.

The most obvious problem is the little time that the bishop has available, and there needs to be serious thinking about his present workload and his responsibilities. The pastoral role of the bishop will need strengthening if he is to be realistically involved in the appraisal process, even if this means removing from him various administrative, bureaucratic duties which are less important. It may only be then that the real ministry of a bishop will be seen and understood:

> The bishop is responsible for the clergy-priests and deacons of his diocese. Here is a basic and vital ministry from which he must never be removed, and yet there is every possible reason for him to overlook it in the multifarious claims upon his time; committees, endlessly in London or Rome, commissions, people to meet, schemes to be organised. Everything which has a place in the Church must be subjected to a rigorous examination in the list of priorities.
>
> (Moore, 1982, p. 169)

The Bishop of Lincoln, for example, sees each of the clergy once every three years for an appraisal of their work. This is seen not to limit the freedom of the clergy but as being done first out of a sense of well-being for the clergy in the diocese of which he is bishop and secondly in order to enable the more effective conduct of the Church's mission. It remains to be seen if that actually happens and if the clergy believe that it does!

The bishops are hoping to improve the life and mission of the Church not only by discussing their work with the clergy, which may remove the accusation of the centre being remote, but in that discussion aiming to improve the morale of the clergy by showing interest in their work. Bishops themselves will not be immune from this task as any honest review of ministry is bound to affect the consideration of their own ministry. The bishop in an appraising situation would do well to adopt an encouraging and positive approach which arises naturally out of his own experience. Any such attempt will fail if the interest is felt to be insincere and one of interference.

What are my hopes and fears about it? The clergy often work alone; some may have spiritual directors or close friends to whom and in whom they confide. Still, a lot of work goes on unrecognized, and in some unrewarding places is taken for granted. To have a formal opportunity of discussing this work with someone could be useful. The vital aspect is that the appraiser be a person of worth and skill who can easily put the appraised at ease whilst at the same time being aware of the appropriate resources, training and statutory agencies that offer expertise on a wide range of subjects. The appraiser will need to act as a clearing house and pass people on to the areas where they can receive the attention they need. He or she will ideally build a relationship of trust over time, and so it is hard to see the interview as being just a formal exercise since it may well develop into an occasion of identifying various areas in which help is needed.

That alone may be the one reason why the bishop may be the most inappropriate person to do all the appraising, all of the time. The appraiser, who will also need training and appraisal, needs to be seen as an enabler rather than just a somewhat threatening manager!

Anything new carries a potential risk of being misunderstood. It is, therefore, vitally important that any schemes which review ministry are introduced carefully, sensitively and with as much discussion as possible. There is a real danger of resentment if a scheme is imposed without meaningful dialogue which will allow for reflection and consolidation. There will be some clergy who will naturally feel very threatened by the whole exercise, and therefore the choice and style of the appraiser needs to be given great consideration, at least in the initial stages.

Not only the style of the interview is important but also the frequency and the venue. In some dioceses variations exist, but on the whole appraisals are either annual or biennial, with a year of action in between. Some bishops who carry out appraisals actually visit the appraised, conducting the interview in his or her own home and involving the spouse. This is highly commendable because any consideration of ministry should not take place without at least some awareness of the ministry situation. It will therefore focus upon the individual whilst naturally taking into account housing, environment, family, etc.

Roy Oswald of the Alban Institute warns against not involving some aspect of the locality:

> Any system that purports to evaluate the clergy without regard to context is a career assessment and not a performance review.
>
> (Oswald, 1990, p. 2)

So providing the appraiser knows the job that is required, has been well-trained, and the venue satisfactorily arranged, the interview could be beneficial not just to the appraised but through him or her to the institution of the Church.

Appraisal can and hopefully will be an effective tool for providing an opportunity to help the clergy adapt to the demands of their job. This could mean less stress and less isolation and more effective pastoral care.

Only time will tell if appraisal fulfils a valuable part of the

Church's ministry. At worst it could divide the clergy from other officers such as bishops and archdeacons, but if so that would be the fault of either the scheme, the appraiser or both! At best it will offer the clergy (and their spouses) the regular opportunity of reflecting upon ministry, setting a few goals if necessary and feeling that the Church officers are genuinely interested in their work. My own heartfelt plea is that *everyone* must take part and be seen to take part or else it will so easily be devalued.

Will anything happen as a result? A cynical answer to this could be that apart from keeping more files on people nothing else would happen although, as Canon Hardaker would seem to imply, appraisal may actually improve the present inadequate record-keeping! That something will happen to those who are appraised is apparent – whether it is good or bad, time will tell.

Appraisal may develop in time a dimension of pastoral care which takes into account the whole person. Such pastoral care doesn't seem to happen at the moment but arises out of a particular demand, usually when there is a crisis of some sort.

If the Church is hoping to encourage appraisal/ministry review then it does so not primarily as a business and promotional exercise but as a theological and practical reflection in the belief that all people are called upon to embark upon the lifelong process of growth towards holiness and wholeness. The Roman Catholic Centre for Human Development believes that this growth towards wholeness and holiness 'involves the total person – spiritual, emotional, physical and intellectual' (Burke, 1985, p. 5).

The Centre not only supports this holistic awareness for everyone but also sponsors an official 'Ministry to Priests' programme. It echoes the American bishops' call that:

> every priest has a right and an obligation to continue his spiritual growth and education. He has a right to strong

support from his superiors, peers, and the people he serves. He also has an obligation to his superiors, and peers, but above all to his people, to continue to grow in grace and knowledge.

(Ibid., p. 6)

The Centre and the Priests programme recognize the integral relationships between the priest's individual spiritual life and the official role of his pastoral duties. Therefore, whatever causes him to grow personally benefits his ministry, and his ministry continually provides him with the opportunity and challenge necessary for true growth. By contrast, whatever causes him not to grow is bound to have an adverse effect on his ministry.

Anglican dioceses, with or without formal appraisal/ministry review schemes, could benefit from the holistic and deeply theological stance taken by the Centre. In comparison with the more individual, tailor-made schemes that are balances between the spiritual, emotional, physical and intellectual, the Church of England schemes appear somewhat lacking theologically.

The huge variety of schemes available is perhaps indicative of a Church that has always aimed to be comprehensive. By being, 'by law established', the official state vehicle of Christianity, the Church of England is under pressure from other professional bodies to adopt professional standards for those in its ministry. Yet it seems to be without a definite theology of ministry upon which to draw. Further, the warning that the present system creates problems needs to be remembered:

> The present structure of the Church creates severe problems for both clergy and Church because it seems to vest care, control and counsel overwhelmingly at one level (the bishop). The result is an authority–pastoral sharing problem. The Church has a very structured hierarchy. This very secular structure of authority, however, poses as an entirely sacred one, creating problems for clergy who have

personal difficulties and clergy who may require advice or counsel.

(Fletcher, 1990, p. 116)

To be committed to a regular ministerial review, particularly with the bishop or one of his senior staff, is to be welcomed only if it allows for reflection and encouragement without interference. The latter would rapidly bring despondency and lessen morale. The former, especially when a spiritual director is also used for the awareness of spiritual growth, should remind the clergy that they belong to a corporate body, and that as representatives of that body their work is taken seriously and with interest. This will then encourage an awareness of self within the context of work.

Ministerial review may well encourage an awareness of this fundamental concept of being dependent upon each other. There is another more vital, dynamic aspect of ministry that appraisal could well seek to encourage an awareness that:

> the ordained priest is called to reflect the priesthood of Christ and to secure the priesthood of the people of God, and to be one of the means of grace whereby God enables the Church to be the Church.
>
> (Ramsey, 1985, p. 111)

To receive this commission holds a responsibility in its exercise, and if it is to be reflected upon demands an even greater responsibility on the person undertaking the review.

If the clergy are in any sense representatives of the Church, and therefore even of God, then to appraise or review their ministry with some competent help may enable 'the mutual sharing of our expertise, to the furtherance of the ministry of others and, in the end, to the extension of the Kingdom of God' (Jacobs, 1989, p. xi).

References

Advisory Council for the Church's Ministry, *The Continuing Education of the Church's Ministry* (ACCM, London, 1980).

E. Anstey, *Staff Appraisal and Development* (Allen & Unwin, London, 1976).

G. Burke, *A Report on Phase One of the Ministry to Priests Programme in the Archdiocese of Cardiff* (The Centre for Human Development, London, 1985).

Flabellum, 'Clergy performance', *Church Observer* (1990).

B. Fletcher, *Clergy Under Stress* (Mowbray, London, 1990).

I. Hardaker, 'Appraising appraisal' (unpublished).

R. Hiscox, J. Gammell and C. Raybould, *Report of the Working Group on Appraisal and Assessment* (ACCM, London, 1988).

M. Jacobs, *Holding in Trust* (SPCK, London, 1989).

L.B. Mead, *Evaluation of, by, for and to the Clergy* (Alban Institute, Washington DC, 1990).

P. Moore, 'Reflections upon reflections' in *Bishops – But What Kind?*, ed. P. Moore (SPCK, London, 1982).

R. Oswald, *Getting a Fix on Your Ministry* (Alban Institute, Washington DC, 1990).

M. Ramsey, *The Christian Priest Today* (SPCK, London, 1985).

G.A. Randell, *Staff Appraisal* (Institute of Personnel Management/Lawrence & Allen, Weston-super-Mare, 1972).

6

A Lay Person's Perception

ELIZABETH SHEDDEN

A puzzling phenomenon occurred as I began my work for this chapter. It was much easier to write the requested biographical description to accompany it than the chapter itself. Then realization dawned. The former asked me to specify my academic history and work interest in the field in the 24 years of my career so far, in order to provide a human interest to the work. It also contained information about the knowledge, competencies and experience that have influenced its production. The latter asked me to give 'a lay person's perception' – a much more diffuse and elusive thing than the specific tale of the unfolding of my academic and professional life so far.

Who is a lay person?　My dictionary of New Testament words is reassuring on this point.[1] *Laos – the people at large* is used in several places in the New Testament to describe the people of God. So, like all baptized Christians, I am one of the people of God, admitted and authorized by my baptism to play my part in the Church. My English dictionary is less reassuring, introducing other possibilities. Am I casual? Placed in a prostrate or recumbent position? Put down? Put in a certain state or position? Laid aside? These are all possible meanings of the word. Or am I one of the people, as distinct from one of the clergy, and therefore a non-professional, not an expert? By now, I am much less comfortable. What I am not seems to be in danger of being much clearer than what I am. That's the trouble with the laity, I hear them say. Who are they, where do they come from, what do they have to offer? You can't look them up in Crockford's – how do you know they can do what you want them to do?

Whose ministry are we developing? My predicament takes us right into the heart of the struggle the Church experiences with its ministry development and appraisal. If it speaks with different voices over its ministry, how can it expect otherwise? Within the Church of England, for example, there is a wide range of opinions. On the one hand we hear that ministry development and appraisal belongs firmly within the three-fold order of bishop, priest and deacon. It is therefore an affair for these ordained professionals to settle between themselves. At the other end of the spectrum we hear that we are all the people of God. Consequently, ministry development and appraisal is an activity for the people of God, as we look together at ministry and mission in any particular context. Its implications are wide-ranging, as we all review together the way in which we are carrying out the awesome responsibilities of membership of the priesthood of all believers. Much energy has been expended already on schemes for mission audit which follow these ideas through into action planning. Each denomination offers its own elucidations and emphases.

Who can appraise who? This situation also leaves unanswered the question as to whether the clergy and lay people can cross the divide between them, engage in an appraisal of one another's gifts and commit themselves to the development of one another's ministry. For some people, lay or ordained, such a process would seem impertinent. For others it seems long overdue. After all, the latter argue, the ministry of the people of God exists in order to prepare God's

81

people for works of service, in order to ensure that we are all equipped to go and make disciples of all nations. With the words of William Temple ringing in their ears, they are concerned to reaffirm that the Church exists for the entire benefit of those outside it. They wish to be released, equipped and empowered to fulfil this call. To them, ministry development and appraisal would be just one part of a logical and necessary process for doing so.

Instead, they often feel trapped, deskilled and disempowered within the Church. How do they talk about this? If they do so, they risk being seen as anti-clerical. If they do not, they risk having their activities prescribed for them without reference to their knowledge and experience. Remember those definitions, 'laid aside', 'put down', 'placed in a recumbent position'?! I think of an experienced lay person fuming over an encounter of this kind. She was a theology graduate and a secondary school teacher, who has since gone on to teach in a theological college. She had been asked by an ordained minister to take over a confirmation class at short notice in order to lead a discussion on the Trinity with a group of teenagers. He had attempted to tell her how to do it. After all, she was lay and not ordained. He had failed to see the knowledge and experience gained in her life so far, and all that she already brought to the task of discussing the Trinity with teenagers.

It is one thing to distinguish between ordained and lay people in order to give appropriate recognition to all that goes into clergy training and ministry development. It is quite another to ignore the range of knowledge and skills which often overlap with training for ordination and ministry development and can almost always inform some aspect of it. It is clear that there are many ways in which the Church has learnt to harness such gifts in a whole range of ways, in both its ecclesiastical structures and its local contexts. Finance committees, parsonage departments, advisory committees, the range of ministry services which exist, all speak to the lay contribution. As they place people in particular positions in relation to their knowledge, gifts and specific tasks that have to be done, the benefits are clear for all to see.

Whose perception do we use?   So much depends on what you see. If you are then to communicate what you see to another, you have quite a task on your hands. Anyone who has tried to sketch will know all that goes into what the dictionary defines as 'the art of representing solid objects on a plane exactly as regards position, shape and dimension as the objects themselves appear to the eye at a particular time'. How much more difficult it is to capture the activity of 'living stones'. In the Church, as a faith community, we each of us work out what we see from where we look. Then, day by day, we are called upon to look at it in another perspective. Interfering with one another's ways of looking or reminding one another, whether lay or ordained, of other ways of seeing, we struggle with a multiplicity of perspectives. At worst, these can be overwhelming. At best, they can help us to share insights that allow the Holy Spirit to disturb us into an unfolding of the gifts and ministries which we all have. Here, we need some of our wisest insights and clearest discernment if we are to make effective use of these gifts.

Harnessing gifts and ministries   There are many exciting examples of the ways in which gifts and ministries are being used. There is no intention of trying to do them justice in a chapter of this kind. Instead, the rest of this chapter looks at three possible approaches which could take us through this multi-faceted context in order to develop our shared understanding of ministry development and appraisal wherever we are. This in its turn will strengthen gifts and ministries.

First, it will be suggested that a more rigorous use of the contributions lay people already make to ministerial development could be fruitful. Secondly, the contribution of appraisal to the development of shared ministry is assessed by means of an example drawn from the professional development scheme of the Lay Ministry Advisers in the diocese of London. Thirdly, the possibility of applying a similar process in a parochial context is examined with a view to fostering the development of shared ministry.

These approaches would all find some resonance in other Churches in the British Isles.

The contribution lay people already make   Many lay people approach the issue of ministerial development and appraisal with considerable knowledge and experience. Conducting my own appraisal with one of the lay members of my committee was revealing and refreshing. He could analyse the particular tools I was using in the light of those he uses regularly. The employment history of most lay people will have included exposure to some form of appraisal. These experiences can be drawn upon in creative ways in order to serve the ministerial development of the clergy.

Nor need such contributions be limited to those people who have experienced appraisal programmes. Lay people already contribute to the ministerial development of their clergy in a myriad of ways. The church was packed on the day of my father's funeral. He had been a prominent lay member of his denomination for many years at local, regional and national levels. That was not the reason for the attendance in such large numbers. He had also become known as 'the minister's friend'. Those with whom he worked could rely on his affectionate support, his forthright challenges and the perspective and encouragement that his reflections gave to their ministry. 'Faithful are the wounds of a friend.'[2]

Give any clergy a few moments to reflect on their ministry so far and they will begin to remember the lay people who told them the truth at important moments, helped them to learn and encouraged their growth. There will be other stories too, of painful and destructive encounters. Yet others, of the patient and triumphant witness of many lay people.

Through the way these people have conducted their lives, the vision for ministry has been kept bright and sharp. Others will have memories of those who have taxed them to the limit and drawn out resources of tact, diplomacy, skill and compassion that they never knew they possessed. It is all good ministerial development!

Designing ways in which lay people could be formally involved in ministerial development and review of clergy is not difficult. There are many approaches which could be drawn upon. Creating a safe context for using such designs is an essential prerequisite. This may at times be more difficult to put in place. The following framework for analysis of some of the information we are seeking may reassure the timid and inspire the confident to see what could be achieved with care, patience and the careful preparation of a suitable approach. Developed over 30 years ago now, it has been tried, tested and adapted in many settings to good effect.

On p. 86 in diagrammatic form we see a way of describing a range of information which exists about any individual as they are relating to others. All the information in Window A is free and open, both to the self and to others. Window B is closed. There is self-knowledge, and though disclosure can be chosen, the window cannot be forced open. Here are our hidden agendas and the private arena of our thoughts and wishes. Window C shows the information with which the poet was so familiar.

> O wad some Power the giftie gie us
> To see ourselves as others see us.

We are often blind to our greatest strengths and our greatest weaknesses. Others can often see them clearly. A process for using the information seen through this window can be a goldmine of treasures for developmental processes.

Window D gives us a reminder of the depths within each of us, unknown to anybody except our Creator. At times, an unexpected revelation will appear in the public arena for

	DATA KNOWN TO SELF	DATA UNKNOWN TO SELF
DATA KNOWN TO OTHERS	A FREE/OPEN	C BLIND TO SELF BUT SEEN BY OTHERS Feedback occurs here
DATA UNKNOWN TO OTHERS	B HIDDEN FROM OTHERS e.g. hidden 'agendas'	D UNKNOWN TO ANYBODY Revelation . . . as things 'pop out' unexpectedly

Disclosure can be chosen, not forced.

Johari's Window (as developed by Luft and Ingram[3])

good or ill. Much of the time, this information remains in the depths. Those who minister need time and help to work on these depths. Persevering prayer, therapy, counselling and other aspects of our life together in the faith community give many of us much needed support in doing so.

These processes, in their turn, nourish the more explicit ones we are examining here.

Luft and Ingram concentrated on Window C. They were concerned to draw attention to the sizes and shapes of the gaps between what we know about ourselves and what others know about us. Once these gaps are identified, they argued, we can develop ways of sharing knowledge in appropriate and helpful ways. When information is there for all to see and not shared, how can we claim to speak the truth in love? If it is shared clumsily, lasting hurt can be inflicted. For Luft and Ingram, the way through these dilemmas was to clarify the principles for the sharing of information. They called it 'feedback'.

The following extract from our professional development programme offers an approach to feedback, which owes much to the approaches their thinking encouraged:

> We get quite a lot of feedback from colleagues, friends and family. Mostly we don't ask for it and are left to guess what it really means. Depending on our state of mind we ignore it, we enjoy it or we concentrate only on the bad bits.
>
> This programme helps us to set out deliberately to get feedback from colleagues with a view to improving our professional performance.
>
> We will get the most out of it if we insist on receiving specific feedback. General statements like, 'You are a really nice person', leave us with a warm feeling but no real idea of what we have done to merit it and, therefore, no opportunity to repeat what we have done well.
>
> Also insist on positive feedback. You can improve from that. It is sometimes useful to know what we do wrong as long as those who give us that information also take the trouble to tell us how we can improve.[4]

Helpful feedback focuses on our behaviour, not just our words. It does not ask 'why?', simply 'what?' It is often a reciprocal activity which needs an atmosphere of mutual trust. It needs to be requested, not offered unasked; timely, as soon as possible after an event; accurate and clear, it requires careful listening and clarifying from those receiving it. It needs to be appropriate, specific, descriptive, usable. Feedback during appraisal is not an excuse to dump unwanted feelings or settle old scores. Rather it is an opportunity for individuals or groups to be honest with one another. Nor do devices for assisting this process have to be complicated. Even the use of a simple sentence completion device can help a group evaluate their relationships in the work that they have done together, over a particular period. It is important to start with positive feedback, in order to help the recipient to listen. The degree of sophistication which one can develop in these evaluation frameworks is endless. Each context will demand its own approach.

Each of us has gifts for which we need to take some responsibility. What can I do? What am I good at? Where am I most effective? What do I enjoy? If we encourage one another to ask questions like these, we can be released more fully into appropriate service. The most simple form of 'ministry development' in which I was involved[5] had five questions in it:

1 What have you been most effective at doing so far in your life?
2 What do you feel comfortable doing?
3 What can't you do?
4 What are the areas where you have been ineffective?
5 Is there a pattern and direction to your life?

Five simple questions, though the conversations following my answers to those questions with a trusted group of friends held the seeds of my next job change.

Two other devices used in training courses were used with great effect for me. One used the simple sentence completion device. Each member of the group who had worked with me over a period had to complete the following three sentences:

1 What I think you do better now is . . .
2 The helpful things you should keep doing are . . .
3 What you do that I find unhelpful is . . .

Each of us had to complete those sentences for one another. The discussions which took place in a safe atmosphere on a reciprocal basis, between a group of people who had built up a great deal of trust, were very fruitful for the management responsibility to which we all returned.[6] Another simple device took place in a Coverdale course.[7] I had to write down all the things that people told me that I did that helped them in the work we had done together. I also had to receive everything they wanted to tell me about what hindered my contribution. The feedback had to be specific, usable, in clear phrases. Through it I built up a very helpful picture of my strengths and weaknesses in the team work of that particular situation.

Such a process can be part of the growth of a whole group. It would not be impossible to imagine a group of lay people, picked because of particular work they had done with clergy in any one year, engaging in an appropriate version of such a process as part of ministry development to the mutual benefit of all concerned.

The cycle of action, reflection and replanning action in the light of that reflection is a familiar component of many effective learning and teaching opportunities. Clear frameworks for feedback offer similar opportunities for growth and change.

So far, this discussion has focused on the developmental benefits of such a process. It is difficult to see how a minister and his or her colleagues can serve to the best of their abilities without such regular reflection and review. I both expect it and seek it from my colleagues and learn continuously through it. There are also important issues of accountability tied into the development of ministry. An increasing number of Anglicans are beginning to understand that we all finance our ministry. This financial responsibility will increase, not decrease in the years ahead. Lay people are used to accountability of all sorts in their own lives. More are beginning to question its absence for their clergy. Is it not part of the responsible stewardship of the Church's financial resources? Surely, they say, appraisal can encourage more effective use of the scarce resources at our disposal. Tasks will be sharpened and responsibilities allocated more appropriately within the faith community.

The contribution of appraisal to the development of shared ministry – an example   Even if we are to refine our frameworks for involving lay people in the ministerial development and appraisal of our clergy, we have only addressed part of the question. We still have to ask whether we are doing enough to draw in the lay contribution to our life together as the people of God. In this section, the experience of the Lay Ministry Advisers in the diocese of London will be described as an example. These advisers are mostly, but not exclusively, lay. They are all employed in order to support and encourage the effective ministry of the people of God. The process used for establishing their work is a familiar one:

1 *What needs to be done?*   The diocesan bishop in Synod, through its Bishop's Council, has been helped to identify certain tasks that need doing, and asked for job descriptions to be formed.

2 *Who can do it?*   The profile of the kind of person who could do a particular job in question has been sketched out. The person specification has been formed. Often this was likely to be a lay person possessing particular professional skills.

3 *How is this person to be retained?*   Practice over appropriate terms and conditions of employment has been developed.

4 *How are they to be supported?* As each role has been filled, questions have been asked about the appropriate management support and consultancy arrangement. Responsibility has been taken for ensuring that these were in place.

By the time I took up my responsibilities, the department was supporting and encouraging six distinct aspects of the ministry of the people of God: adult education, children's education, youth education, pastoral and family education, readers, stewardship.

Ecclesiastical managers have plenty to do, in simply ensuring that continuing and satisfactory answers to all the needs and issues listed above are provided. In addition, they also need to consider another group of questions. How is work reviewed and developed in the light of the experience being gained? What processes are in place for measuring knowledge and competence? How is competence to be increased and knowledge expanded?

There is a danger that professional development and in-service training possibilities are sought in the light of individual foibles or interests. Is it not preferable, first, to reaffirm and clarify what knowledge base is needed for a particular role; second, to assess the competencies needed in order to be effective in the role; and third, to assess what degree of competence a post-holder has achieved and to review it regularly? Once that process has been followed, in-service training needs emerge that can be closely related both to the task in hand and the needs, if not always the wishes, of the individual! Scarce resources can be used in a more disciplined way and precious budgets for in-service training allocated more strategically.

One way of working on this issue would be to obtain the consultancy services of an experienced professional in the field of appraisal. This we were able to do.[8] From his knowledge of the Church as well as his experience in designing such systems within the Christian context, he worked with us to get something in place which would separate out for us the key aspects of knowledge, skill and competence each adviser needed in order to do the job.

The following introduction written for the scheme helps to capture some of the important principles behind its development:

> Development implies some form of appraisal.
>
> However, appraising someone is not easy. The 'outsider' sees so little of the game and is not, in the nature of things, a specialist.
>
> The only 'expert' is the individual Adviser/Officer who is doing the job. Each person is working in a unique way.
>
> ### PURPOSES
>
> The purposes of this appraisal are:
>
> - To enable each member of the department to recognise her or his own individual strengths
> - To help us to make the best use of those strengths
> - To help recognise where development is needed
> - To identify what training and education individuals and teams need.
>
> ### STANDARDS
>
> A programme of this kind will benefit both the members of the department and the Diocese by increasing our competence and confidence.
>
> We shall be better able to say what work is going well and what needs to be improved.
>
> It will give us valuable data when competing for Diocesan budget allocation.
>
> It will enable us to meet uninformed criticism from the Diocese.
>
> ### OUR PROGRAMME
>
> This appraisal has three elements: self-appraisal, help from colleagues who, where possible, know our work and, finally, an interview with me.
>
> Whilst we are all specialists, there are functions which are common to all of us and interests we all share.

Seven of these have been chosen:

- The Adviser/Officer as Administrator
- The Adviser/Officer as Consultant
- The Adviser/Officer as Trainer and Educator
- The Adviser/Officer as Advocate
- The Adviser/Officer as Stress Manager
- The Adviser/Officer as Specialist
- The Professional who is also a Christian.

ACCURACY

This approach to appraisal helps everyone to make a reasonably accurate assessment of their current state of understanding and competence in the chosen common areas. In addition to this, there will be a section for their own specialism for which they will have provided their own material.

HOW IT WORKS

1 Each member of the department (including me) will have a set of papers including your specialist section.
2 We will make our assessment of ourselves according to the scale:

   5 Highly competent in this area
   4 Adequately competent in this area
   3 Some competence but attention needed
   2 Urgent improvement needed in this area
   1 Serious deficiencies in this area – immediate consultation with manager.

3 We get colleagues who know us and what we do, either at first hand or – if that is not possible – by repute, to sit with us and rate according to the same scale, explaining the ratings to us. Also there will be differences of interpretation, it is important to know what they are. We may need different colleagues for different sections.
4 We use these two sets of ratings as the basis for our annual appraisal interview with our manager (in my case the chairperson of the Committee, in yours – a meeting with me).
5 Please remember this is not an exam, or competition. You

cannot fail, pass, lose or win. This is intended as an aid in your professional development.

THE SPECIALIST SECTION

Those who work in teams within the department will probably want to check out their specialist section with each other before arriving at the elements which need assessing.[9]

Content and process It is worth noting that there were certain crucial aspects to the introduction of the scheme. Every effort was made to ensure that the knowledge and skills to be measured were described in as specific a way as possible and that they were measurable in some way. A scoring system was devised which was clear and simple to use. Great attention was paid to the process of establishing the scheme. A draft framework was brought to the staff group and discussed in some detail. Time was given to each specialism in order to help staff formulate their specialist sections. Particular care was taken with the whole issue of 'feedback' and 'competence', drawing on some of the principles enunciated earlier. For example, a definition of competence was offered in addition to the description on feedback to which we referred earlier:

> The foregoing papers depend, in the skills section, upon the concept of 'competence'. It is important to say both what competence is and what it is not since the word is so often misused. Perhaps the best way to describe what we mean is to say how we recognise competent people in our field.

COMPETENT PEOPLE

1 Set realistic goals and work effectively towards them. .
2 Have an overall view of what needs to be done and act accordingly.
3 Foresee the implications of their actions upon clients and upon other professionals and situations.
4 Seek feedback and use it to improve their performance.

5 Set realistic goals for continuous professional development.

6 Contribute to the effectiveness of their clients.

COMPETENCE DOES NOT IMPLY PERFECTION

When we say someone is competent, or even highly competent, we are referring to their professional performance. We are not making a statement about their worth.[10]

When all the specialist sections had been refined a pilot programme was established. After further adjustment, it was established for regular use on an annual basis.

Outcomes There have been several positive outcomes. In-service training plans can be clarified more clearly. The development of skills can be measured by advisers and director together. The process helped one member of staff to leave in order to pursue a change of direction, having realized that the existing job was the wrong one in the long term, though it had been an important stepping stone in the short term.

By far the most interesting outcome was that the development of the specialist pages of the scheme enriched and expanded the understanding of adviser, peer and director alike, as to the nature of the task being undertaken. In specific terms, the process enabled us to ensure that job descriptions were reviewed and refined regularly. This is not simply a bureaucratic exercise. Such reviews feed directly back into the mission and ministry of the wider Church. As the bishop in Synod declares: 'we need to ensure that . . .', the advisers can say: 'and we are assisting that process through the following tasks we undertake in the following ways'. Such thinking and planning contribute to the underpinning of the work on pastoral planning which is going on across the diocese at the moment through Agenda for Action.[11]

This year, we are planning the relicensing of all our Readers.[12] They too take part in an appraisal process, through the use of detailed questionnaires to them and their incumbents. These questionnaires have been designed and refined each time they are used by a representative group of Readers working with me.

In the diocese we have lay chaplaincy schemes.[13] One of these schemes too is being encouraged to develop its own appraisal scheme, using a similar process.

The parochial context   Each parish here is working on its Mission Action Plan at the moment in order to contribute to the pastoral plan for the diocese. It is encouraging to be part of such strategic thinking. One key element to the process is the deployment of stipendiary clergy. Yet they cannot and should not be our only consideration. All the people of God need to be deployed in such a way that their gifts and ministries are used to the benefit of all in the task of making disciples. Some parishes have shown great imagination and verve in ensuring the paid employment of lay people as part of their mission and ministry teams. All involve lay people in a range of voluntary tasks. The advisers each play a part in this through a range of educational and training devices and resources. There is still much to be done in order to develop networks across the diocese for using voluntary endeavour more fruitfully. No doubt the same is true across the whole Church.

By what authority?   It is important to ensure that lay people who are employed by the Church are 'owned' by the Church. It is also helpful to commission and authorize them in appropriate ways. This may be for a parochial position or for a role in a wider Church. However, the giving of positional authority does not of itself confer any sapiential authority. Even when sapiential authority exists, it needs to be nurtured and refreshed. Appraisal processes such as those described above can be adapted in order to contribute in some way to the development of knowledge and competence.

Paid or unpaid? However, as the examples from Reader
and lay chaplaincy appraisal indicate, you do not need to be
employed by the Church to have your ministry appraised or
appraise it yourself. Each member of the faith community
can benefit from it. How do we develop such reviews and
appraisals together for every member of the Church?

Do we need to do so? We all long to become more confident
Christians capable of integrating our faith and our life
wherever we find ourselves. There are a variety of elements
to this: being rooted in the life of God; being members of a
Christian community that is in touch with its local context,
who are bringing refreshment to the life in that context. The
suggestion here is that it is much easier to do so if we are
aware of our gifts and the value of our experience. Equipping, enabling and empowering the people of God requires
us to give time to the development and harnessing of each
contribution. For as the apostle Paul reminds us: 'From him,
the whole body, joined and held together by every supporting ligament, grows and builds itself up in love, *as each part
does its work.*'[14]

Some challenging consequences for leadership

Hiddenness Those of us who spend time in ensuring that
the ministry of the people of God is effective have some
interesting issues to face over our own roles. I can remember
saying to one of the new members of our Diocesan Com-
munications Team: 'Mine is a hidden role, I am rarely seen
in public.' There was some truth in the jest. Often the key
task is 'holding the ring' in order to facilitate the use of the
experts in the team. Supporting and enabling them, acting
as the catalyst to them in the development of their skills, is
essentially a hidden role, the exact opposite of public
attempts at omnicompetence which have dogged some
developments in the ministry.

Support Ministry development and appraisal cannot be provided in isolation. It is merely part of the infrastructure we need to have for equipping the Church in order to ensure that we can fulfil our mission. Other significant elements in the development of a fully collaborative and shared ministry include systems for the support and supervision of clergy and lay people alike, and ways of providing the pastoral help we need in critical moments. It takes all the inventiveness we can muster and plenty of hard work in order to create a culture in which there are circles of care where we can flourish:

> It is a call to conversion and community . . . to perceiving the church as a communion of persons in relation, where faith is both surely founded but also is a daily risk, where living with questions is no longer threatening and undermining, but rather the way in which we are enabled to be drawn more deeply into the mystery of God's eternal purposes for us. In short, we are committed to each other as we journey together into the future.[15]

Letting go It is clearly not enough to set up a context where gifts are discerned unless that context also enables gifts to be used once they have been discerned. Sadly, it is here that many lay people report a sense of the shoe pinching. They sharpen their awareness of their gifts, they become involved in training courses of various kinds and become more and more equipped for a whole range of ministries. They find then, that even after all this, somehow there is no place in which these gifts can be used. Disappointed, they move into other contexts. These may be Churches where the ministry of the whole people of God is taken more seriously, or other contexts altogether. Though these are undoubtedly enriched, the Church can be the poorer.

Ministry development and appraisal will be much more strongly identified with the growth of our awareness of shared and collaborative ministry if we are prepared to take a view of the role of the clergy which emphasizes their role as co-ordinators and enablers and leaders of others into ministry. This may require skills which their training never gave them. It also asks them to celebrate and affirm a wide range of gifts other than their own, and see where their distinctive contribution fits into the pattern of service. It requires them to have at their fingertips a wide range of techniques for doing so. It asks them to develop the skills for ensuring that such techniques are used wisely and sensitively. Outcomes will include facing criticism for allowing people to do things that have been traditionally clergy tasks. There are risks. Trusting people to do things you could have done yourself gives you the taxing constraint of making professional judgements at one remove. Hours will need to be spent on training people to think through the issues for themselves, and encouraging them to argue with us, so that approaches can be constantly challenged and refined. And then, after all exchanges, we need to be both delighted and humbled that often the most creative interventions of all will come from the simplest and most unlikely of sources.

Certain assumptions Such a working culture is underpinned by certain assumptions. There is an interdependence which encourages people to be open with one another in order to be more effective. All work needs to be reported upon in some way. Accountability again! Mutual respect for one another's different skills and functions needs to be established. Can we really believe we are of equal worth, but have different functions? Can we learn to value one another equally, irrespective of the price tag or status others put on us? There is struggle – some of the sharpest and toughest arguments take place in shared ministry teams! There is a team-building game in which all are given some jigsaw pieces. If the pieces are pooled a picture can be made. The struggle is always over who can give the first pieces away in order to ensure that the picture is made co-operatively.

My own appraisal was completed recently. It was heartening to discover the things that came more easily to me now. It was a little depressing to be reminded of the things that I had found more difficult to change. Best of all was that at the end of the time, plans were laid for my own professional development and the development of the department. Definite goals were in place and there was work to be done. 'You did not choose me, but I chose you', said the Lord, 'and appointed you to bear much fruit.'[16] It is my hope that the attention which has been given to ministerial development and appraisal will not be a cause of fear and anxiety but will in fact increase the fruit-bearing of which we are all capable within the Body of Christ.

References

1   W.E. Vine, *Expository Dictionary of New Testament Words* (Marshall Pickering, London, 1952).

2   Proverbs 27.6.

3   Luft and Ingram, *Effective Feedback* (1955).

4   Professional Development Scheme, Lay Ministry Department, Diocese of London, 1991.

5   Developed by N.C. Marston when Development Officer in Northants Social Services Department. Currently Director of Training for the Archdiocese of the Indian Ocean.

6   T. Scott, when tutor of the Management and Planning course at the National Institute of Social Work.

7   Coverdale Organization, *A Systematic Approach to Team Work* (1991).

8   The Revd Derrick Rowland was the Board officer responsible for the Scheme for Professional Development for trainees and consultants run by the General Synod Board of Education. He has had experience of establishing appraisal systems over the past decade in a number of settings and has worked with several dioceses in the establishment of appraisal for clergy.

9   As note 4.

10 As note 4.

11 *Agenda for Action: The Way Ahead for the Diocese of London* (1992).

12 Questionnaires for Relicensing of Readers – Diocese of London (1993).

13   Appraisal Scheme: Lay Chaplaincy.
14   Ephesians 4.16.
15   The Rt Revd and Rt Hon. Dr David Hope, Bishop of London,
         from the presidential address to the Diocesan Synod, 29
         October 1991, pp. 8–9.
16   John 15.16.

7

A Bishop's Perspective

JEREMY WALSH

Bishops take very seriously the phrase 'Your care – and mine', in the Institution service. They recognize the major responsibility that this places on them, not only for what we loosely refer to as 'pastoral care' – of both clergy and parishes – but also for ministerial development. They try to be easily available for the clergy, probably as never before. With responsibility for appointments always high on the agenda of every bishop's staff meeting, they need to know their clergy well, so that gifts, experience and personality can be matched to the needs and traditions of each parish or specialist appointment. They will often be asked to write references for other bishops and patrons.

The hierarchical model   Some have therefore set up programmes of appraisal and development in which they are personally and very fully involved, sharing this responsibility with their senior staff. The chief objection to such a programme is the amount of time required to operate an effective process of appraisal, when this has to be done in competition with all the other demands on the diary. A diocese with 200 clergy is likely to have two bishops and two archdeacons. If they alone are to conduct the appraisal interviews, and everyone is to be seen annually, each must interview 50 every year. For the appraisal programme to be anything like a rigorous process, the time for preparation, travelling, interviewing and follow-up is likely to average at least five hours – a huge commitment, even for workaholics! It is easy to start on such a programme with great enthusiasm, only to be defeated by this time demand.

There is a particular problem for the diocesan bishop. How should he participate in the programme? For the programme to be most effective, the interview process needs continuity and the steady build-up of trust over the years. If the diocesan bishop works with only one in four of his clergy, seeing them every year, how would this be viewed by the others, and what effect will it have on his relationship with them? If he sees a different group each year, continuity of contact is lost, and although he can overcome this to some extent by reading the records prepared by his colleagues, the clergy themselves may find it unsatisfactory.

Limitations   In deciding whether or not to implement a hierarchical appraisal scheme, there are a variety of other issues to be considered. How will it be perceived by those taking part? Is it expected to be compulsory? Will clergy be inhibited by having, as they may see it, to 'bare their souls' to bishops and archdeacons? Will the process raise expectations (about future appointments, for example) that cannot be fulfilled? Will everyone be clear about the purpose? Do all bishops and archdeacons have the necessary skills for this particular work, let alone the time available?

We live in a world where regular appraisal is an accepted feature of an individual's working life, particularly in industry and the services. Managers and other senior employees are accountable for their performance, and the lines of accountability are clearly laid down. Many lay people expect the Church to operate in this way, and when they perceive performance to be inadequate they may well inform the bishop, so that he can remedy the situation. In doing so, they credit him with powers which he does not have. At the Institution, he invests a new incumbent 'with all the rights and duties of the benefice, and the cure of souls of the parishioners', and this gives him the freehold of the living. Nothing is said about accountability, and nothing is implied, even by the oath of canonical obedience.

We may or may not wish it otherwise, but this is the way it is. The Church may seem to be very much like a bank, with branches on prime corner sites in almost every community, but the clergy are not branch managers, answerable to the bishop for the way in which they work, as if he were an area or district manager. They have an almost unlimited freedom, and unlike most managers in industry they can only be transferred if they choose to accept a new appointment offered them. (The bishop has no more power to transfer the branch manager than he has to close the local branch!)

This limits the bishop's ability to initiate a compulsory appraisal scheme; everything must be done by agreement. This is no bad thing, but it can be a major limitation. Some clergy at least are likely to see hierarchical appraisal as interference with their freedom, and be very resistant to it. Moreover, they may well find it difficult to be completely open and frank with those who are likely to be concerned with their future appointments. (Appraisal is still so often seen in negative terms, as if it was more to do with exposing faults and failures than with identifying gifts and successes.) This was one reason why we chose a non-hierarchical scheme for our first introduction of appraisal to the Gloucester diocese.

Benefits Sadly, the thing that worries most clergy about hierarchical appraisal is the very thing that could be of greatest long-term benefit to them. When a bishop is asked for a reference, he is often acutely aware of his lack of accurate knowledge of an individual. If he knew more about them, his references might actually be more affirming, not less. Often gifts and skills are unknown or inadequately recognized. The bishop may know little in detail about

Continuing Ministerial Education (CME) work that has been done, or extra-parochial activities undertaken. He may be over-conscious of letters of criticism he has received, because it is more often the aggrieved rather than the satisfied who write to him. We often have to evaluate the clergy's work on very flimsy evidence, and our perceptions are easily coloured by haphazard conversations.

If, as a result, our references are inadequate, clergy may not be offered appointments which could suit them ideally; on the other hand, if we write over-generously they can find themselves in posts for which they are not really suited – a recipe for future unhappiness. We do need to know our clergy better, and direct participation in the appraisal process could be a tremendous benefit.

Clarifying the purpose   Yet it can also raise expectations which cannot be fulfilled. Although pastoral reorganization has led to the suspension of presentation in many benefices, the bishop's patronage is still severely limited by our inherited system of appointments. If the purpose of an appraisal scheme is seen as related to future appointments, the bishop (or archdeacon) may unwittingly engender hopes which cannot be fulfilled because there are no suitable posts at his disposal. This suggests that care needs to be taken so that this is *not* seen as the appraisal's main purpose. The chief objective must always be the enhancement of an individual's ministry in the place where that person is already working, and this purpose must be made very clear at the outset.

However, if we are primarily seeking to help clergy become more effective ministers in their existing posts, it immediately becomes easier for bishops to delegate much of the appraisal process to other people. In some places, rural deans have been involved in a kind of 'line management' capacity. This reduces the detailed involvement of bishops and archdeacons, who can then work with each other and with senior members of the diocesan staff, which requires a much more limited time commitment. The rural deans can

105

work with the other clergy in their deaneries. One implication of working in this way is that rural deans have to be chosen with this work in mind, and it can involve a major change in their relationship with their fellow clergy. Because they are not 'line managers' but *primus inter pares*, other clergy may well find it difficult to accept them in the appraisal role, and any scheme which involves them needs to be introduced with the greatest care. However, working through rural deans has met with reasonable success in some places, and it may well be the most appropriate way forward if hierarchical appraisal is to become the future norm, despite the obvious difficulties. One particular difficulty is the question of compulsion, for not only does compulsion sit uneasily with a parochial system which is staffed by freehold incumbents, but there are almost bound to be certain clergy in any deanery who will find it difficult to work with the rural dean, however carefully he has been chosen with this work in mind.

The Gloucester approach   When we began thinking about appraisal in my own diocese there was no desire on the part of our bishops and archdeacons to operate a hierarchical system. On the other hand, there was a need to promote CME more effectively, and to try and introduce a more systematic and consumer-orientated approach to it. This led us in the direction of appraisal, but to a non-hierarchical scheme. It happened that I was also CME Officer, and clearly my other responsibilities would severely limit the time available for this work. I needed help, and I had to be prepared to delegate. I gathered together a group of clergy to discuss with them how this might best be done.

A number of principles began to emerge. Perhaps the most important was that each of the clergy should take responsibility for their own CME. It was therefore not my job, as CME Officer, or anyone else's, to tell them what to do. Accepting personal responsibility is, of course, a most important general principle, but we recognized its particular relevance for CME within the context of independent freehold incumbencies. Our task would be helping people to identify their educational and training needs, to work out what CME would be most appropriate for them, and then to carry their chosen programme through.

We saw that this would mean, primarily, helping them build on their strengths, develop their recognizable gifts and foster their special interests. We were to encourage, not to find fault or expose weaknesses, even if there was also a need to help them identify those things they do less well, in order to improve their all-round effectiveness in ministry.

Consultancy This led us to plan a consultancy scheme, using our own diocesan clergy as consultants, who would visit clergy in their homes and invite them to work through a simple process of self-appraisal, with CME as the clear objective. There would be no hidden agendas, and no reporting back to the bishop; the visits would be entirely confidential. Once the CME needs had been identified, the clergy would be given information about CME opportunities, and it would be up to them to get in touch with the CME Officer when they wanted financial help from the CME fund. (We operate on the 1 per cent of stipend principle for funding, allowing its use in as flexible a way as possible to enable sabbaticals and other more expensive projects to be financed.)

We realized early on that the consultants would need training if their work was to be effective, so we invited Derrick Rowland, at that time Adult Education Officer with the Church of England Board of Education, to help us in this way. His experience and skill has been invaluable, and he continued to be the external consultant to the scheme when he left the Board of Education to work with the Coverdale Organization. Not only has he trained our consultants but he has also acted as facilitator at each of our annual conferences, when we have worked together as a group on the planning and development of our scheme.

It has, from the start, been a corporate enterprise, and

all decisions have been taken by consensus. The consultants have developed a strong sense of fellowship in the work, and of 'owning' the scheme itself, and have always made the annual conference a very high priority. From the initial planning conference onwards, we have worked together at the way we wanted to do things, often down to quite small details.

Contracts   An important element was the contract each consultant would have with the CME Officer. What exactly was expected of them? How many 'clients' would each have to visit? (We wish we could find a better word to describe the clergy we work with!) How frequently should visits be made? How would expenses be reimbursed? For how long were they committing themselves to this work? And so on. The group decided on the terms of the contract and were then invited to be a consultant on those terms. From time to time the contract has been revised as the scheme has changed and developed, but it has always been a corporate decision. Contracts of this nature have a lot to commend them, so that everyone involved knows where they stand. Far too often the Church asks people to take on work without getting mutual expectations sorted out in advance.

Once consultants have met their clients for the first time, an early task is to negotiate a simple contract with them, to ensure that both consultant and client have the same expectations of the process. We produced a very simple leaflet on the scheme and circulated it to all the clergy, but with around 200 clergy in the diocese and only ten consultants, we had to decide which clergy to target with our initial invitations to participate in the scheme. Four key groups emerged: those just finishing their post-ordination training; those in their first incumbencies; clergy coming into the diocese; and those who had already expressed an interest in taking part. The consultants themselves had to go through the process before offering it to others, so we launched the scheme by writing to some 20 other clergy. As time went on, each consultant added new clients to their lists, up to an agreed maximum of ten, and later the consultant group was enlarged, but we decided quite deliberately to make haste slowly.

The names of clergy to be approached were selected by the CME Officer and checked with each consultant to make sure that they were happy to take the individuals on. Just occasionally there was a mis-match, but these were few and far between. As bishop-in-charge, I then wrote to the prospective clients explaining the scheme, and telling them that I had asked their particular consultant to visit them. Refusals have been almost non-existent, although it has to be admitted that our chosen groups were all of clergy who were likely to be interested. I have often been asked if the scheme is compulsory. My answer has been 'Yes and no'. Yes, the invitation to take part came from me, until I gave up being CME Officer, and it therefore had a little episcopal weight behind it. I took the initiative and we did not simply wait for clergy to opt in. But no, it is not compulsory, for clergy can decline to see a consultant, and even if they do they are not obliged to do any CME. That has remained their own responsibility, and the decisions are theirs. Consultants reported back to me only that they had visited; they did not tell me what had been suggested or agreed.

Guide to Self-Appraisal   Before visiting, the consultant sent out our *Guide to Self-Appraisal*. The group has revised it once or twice, but it was always more or less in this very simple form:

Ministry
Considering your ministry over the last three years:

- What have been the highlights?
- Which part of your ministry do you like best?
- Which part of your ministry do you like least?

Goals

Considering such aspects as duties, responsibilities, workload, family, leisure, facilities, help from the diocese, finance, assistance and co-operation from colleagues, shared ministry, etc.:

- What are your goals for the next year or two?
- What would you like to see added to or omitted from your work so that these goals could be achieved?
- As you reflect on your goals, which need greater priority?

Vocation

In the light of your present vocation:

- What is your vision for the future?
- What do you find fulfilling in your ministry?
- How are you continuing to develop spiritually?

CME

- What skills training, educational opportunity or other help do you need in developing yourself in your ministry?

This formed the basis for each consultation. Sometimes the CME could be readily identified; sometimes a further visit became necessary. There were other topics of conversation, too. For some clergy, the visit provided an opportunity to let off steam, or to unload a variety of personal problems on to someone who had come from outside the parish. The consultant group had anticipated this, and recognized that it would often be hard to set boundaries to the discussion. While they could not accept responsibility for continuing pastoral care, they have been able to encourage clergy and to suggest ways of resolving their difficulties, providing a valuable listening ear and then pointing them towards other help that is available.

We thought initially that the consultants would need support groups, and set up a network – small groups of them who were to get together from time to time to share experiences and difficulties. This never worked. It was just one more meeting to attend, and the annual conference pro- vided sufficient mutual support. From the start, some of the consultants have been women, and later we were able to bring in some non-stipendiary clergy, as well as offering them the scheme itself.

Consultancy principles Last year, the group agreed their Principles of Consultancy:

1 All clients are voluntary in all aspects and at all stages of the CME scheme.
2 The relationship between consultant and client is con- fidential in all aspects.
3 All appraisal is affirmatory, especially as clients are volun- tary. The appraisal is to build on strengths, rather than concentrate on weaknesses.
4 Consultants must undergo the full process themselves, as must a CME Officer offering consultancy.
5 Ownership of the CME process lies with the consultants, including the CME Officer and the bishop responsible.
6 New consultants have to be accepted by the current con- sultants, the CME Officer and the bishop responsible.
7 (a) The role of consultants, as consultants, is limited. It is not pastoral. If consultants become aware of other problems they should, as appropriate, encourage the client to seek help.
  (b) If a consultant, exceptionally, is prepared to offer the help, it must be made clear that this is not part of the CME consultation and should be offered for a separate occasion.
8 Consultants experiencing any problem in consulting with a client should seek the mutual support of the CME Officer and/or one or more consultants, other than their own CME consultant.
9 (a) Consultants are not messengers between clients and

anyone else, be they bishops, CME Officer or providers of education and training.

(b) Accordingly, it is not part of consultancy to organize
clients' CME. Clients do that, as part of owning it. It
is fundamental that clients be helped to take responsibility for their own CME.

From time to time consultants had to drop out of the scheme.
Some moved out of the diocese, and others found the
workload too much. At the same time, we wanted to extend
the scheme to more clergy than the initial consultant group
could cope with.

Increasing the number presented difficulties. Joining an
existing group is never easy, and new members would have
to accept a scheme they had not shared in planning. We took
great care in choosing together the clergy to be invited, and
under Derrick Rowland's guidance we worked hard at the
process of 'steering and joining'. Joiners need time to
understand and digest ideas which other people have already
been working on; steerers know the reasons for decisions
previously taken and may resent having to take time to
explain them. They may resent even more strongly a joiner
challenging a decision, or suggesting an alternative. Special
conferences, where prospective new consultants could be
thoroughly briefed, given some initial training and invited to
accept the contract with the CME Officer, were essential and
invaluable. Good integration does not happen by accident,
and it is something we seldom give much thought or attention to in Church life, for example, when new members are
elected to a PCC, or a new person joins the bishop's staff.

As time went on, the consultant group began to realize the
limitations of the basic *Guide to Self-Appraisal*. It was adequate
for a first, and probably a second, visit but what then? I
raised this question with the group at one of our annual consultations. It happened that I was going down with 'flu and
had to go home and retire to bed after the opening session.
Left to themselves, the group decided that we needed a much

more highly developed appraisal process and immediately set about planning it. (Had I been too restraining an influence?)

Professional Development Scheme The Professional Development Scheme (PDS) which was the outcome was initially written for us by Derrick Rowland and then worked on thoroughly by the whole consultant group until it reached its present form. Like the earlier process, the consultants have used it with each other before offering it to their clients.

The PDS has eight sections, which do not have to be used all at once but can be worked at over a period of time. They cover pastoral care, spiritual life, liturgy, management, education, mission, 'the whole person', and special interests. (There is a supplement for sector ministers, dealing with their special concerns.) Under each heading, a number of questions are raised, and the individual is invited to rate his or her skills according to a scale from 'Highly aware' to 'Room for improvement'.

Experience shows that we tend to undervalue ourselves and get inaccurate or inadequate feedback from other people, so that we find it difficult to make an accurate assessment of our skills. The process therefore involves the use of colleagues – other ministers or lay people who know the individuals well, and chosen by them. The colleague is invited to go through the same questions and put down a rating. Individual and colleague then sit down together and compare their assessments. Where there are differences these can be discussed, and the ratings can then be revised, whether up or down. (Different colleagues may be appropriate for different sections.)

Goals The consultant then returns to help the individual reflect on the results, and assists in working out realistic goals for future development and training. As with the initial scheme, the process is entirely confidential. Its purpose is to help improve ministry and not to provide information for the bishop, but a form is provided so that individuals can send him information to be included in their personal files if they choose to do so.

The PDS is not simply work-orientated, as the section on 'The Whole Person' makes clear. These are some of the questions in this section:

	Assessment	
	Self	Colleague
Do you:		
1 allocate appropriate work time?	_____	_____
2 reserve time (where appropriate) for spouse and children?	_____	_____
3 spend time with your wider family?	_____	_____
4 establish and maintain friendships?	_____	_____
5 pay attention to your health?	_____	_____
6 allocate time for leisure interests?	_____	_____
7 take proper recreation:		
• taking your 'day off'?	_____	_____
• taking holidays?	_____	_____
• working 'reasonable' hours?	_____	_____

This is the typical style in which the questions in each section are set out, raising a whole variety of issues which ministers ought to take seriously.

It is early days to assess the value of the PDS; of some 120 in the original scheme, only 30 have so far moved on to the PDS. In due course we shall collect feedback, with a view to its eventual revision.

Ask about policy in the Church of England, and you will get 44 different answers. Dioceses are all very different, and although our independence probably leads us to spend far too much time re-inventing the wheel, there are many good reasons for taking an independent line. Our personal preferences, experience and theological outlook inevitably and quite properly come into play. We inherit different traditions, and operate in varied circumstances, so something which works well elsewhere will not necessarily suit us. Nor can we simply take another's programme and use it; we have to adapt and mould it to suit our own particular situations and priorities. I have not attempted here a systematic survey of the work being done by bishops in other dioceses; I have simply written out of my own experience, concentrating mainly on the way in which we have developed an appraisal scheme in the diocese of Gloucester during the past six years or so, and our reasons for choosing to do it our particular way.

The bishop's role I am sure the consultants would agree that it has been good to have the suffragan bishop closely involved in our process, although once the scheme was up and running, one of the consultants took over the role of CME Officer. My initial participation helped to secure recognition of the scheme, and to get it firmly established as a normal expectation among clergy in the diocese. It also ensured that the consultants recognized that their work is genuinely valued. No scheme can function effectively without the wholehearted support and backing of the diocese's bishops.

As participants in the PDS gain the confidence to share the results of their appraisal work with the bishop, he will gain valuable information when it comes to making appointments, writing references and overseeing an individual's career development. From time to time issues will arise during the process which consultants can encourage their clients to talk over with the bishop. Ministerial development is a fundamental part of our 'care'; it will never be easy for a bishop to give it adequate time, even when assisted by his senior staff, but with a programme like the Gloucester scheme he will know that it is being encouraged, through an officially delegated programme, and clergy will feel that their gifts and skills, and their expectations and hopes, are being taken seriously by him.

8

Spirituality and Appraisal

TREVOR WILLMOTT

> Spirituality recognises the way we are with ourselves and the way we are with other people. *But* above all it depends on the way we are with God.
>
> (Sydney Evans)

The Christian faith is a unity in which all its distinct and different parts belong together. If any one part is allowed to become dominant or separated, it soon begins to die away. As Christians we believe that God seeks to relate to our whole being, and the only human response to his act of grace is from the whole. John Macquarrie, in his book *Paths in Spirituality*, states:

> There are three major factors combined together in the living unity of the Christian religion: doctrine, worship, and deeds. The strength of the Christian religion is this complex texture embracing the whole of human life. Together they form something that can stand up to the greatest strains without giving way. But if we allow the strands to become separated, then any one of them in isolation begins to show weaknesses, and will not maintain itself.

This statement seems to me to have much to say to any handbook on ministry development and appraisal. An appraisal principle which lacks theological/doctrinal

116

rationale will soon become a system of personnel management. Equally, an appraisal system which is not concerned with the 'whole person under God', i.e. the recollecting or gathering together in prayer and worship of the self in a moment of encounter with the living God, denies the God-given opportunity for the transformation of the person into the likeness of Christ.

An appraisal system ought rightly to raise questions about the relationship between the professional and personal life of those engaged in ministry. It should call for a careful exploration of the connections between ministry and spirituality – a spirituality which lies at the root of our vocation. In my own work as a spiritual director I am brought into contact with those who have often separated ministry from spirituality, the doing from the being under God. It is no accident that the annual appraisal of those within the first three years of ordained ministry too often highlights the fact that in the 'busy-ness' of ministry, the frenetic activity which overtakes many clergy, one of the first areas to suffer is that of personal prayer. Prayer too easily becomes the last thing on the ever-increasing agenda of people-centred ministry. Corporate worship, instead of being the focus of the whole life, both of the individual and the community, becomes another burden often because it is not undergirded by that personal prayer relationship which for many, if not all, clergy lies at the heart of their vocation to ordination. Prayer becomes something for the future – a retreat which never occurs. To put the problem another way: the pattern of spirituality/prayer which an appraisal system displays is a clear indication of the worked-through integration of the role and the person.

Theophan the Recluse points this out most forcefully:

> Prayer is the test of everything; prayer is also the source of everything; prayer is the driving force of everything; prayer is also the director of everything. If prayer is right, everything is right. For prayer will not allow anything to go wrong.

117

In defining spirituality, Sydney Evans suggests three areas
of focus:

- The way we are with ourselves.
- The way we are with others.
- The way we are with God.

In addressing the theme of spirituality and appraisal, I take
those three headings.

The way we are with ourselves   Do you believe, so far as
you know your own heart, that God has called you to the
office and work of a deacon or of a priest in his Church?

> We trust that long ago you began to weigh and ponder all
> this, and that you are fully determined, by the grace of God,
> to give yourselves wholly to his service.
>
> (ASB Ordinal)

The way we are with ourselves demands that we both know
ourselves and are prepared to work with that knowledge. In
my work as a Diocesan Director of Ordinands I encourage
every prospective candidate to write his or her own faith
audit. The audit is a way of self-recollection which seeks to
do justice to all that has hitherto been in a person's life.
Three questions address each five-year period:

1 Who was I? Who was the person I knew then and what
  made him or her tick?
2 Where was the world? The context in which I found myself
  – the individuals, the communities, the issues which gave
  substance to my growth?
3 Where was God? How did I know, experience, respond to
  him? Where were the times when he seemed absent or I
  too busy or involved to be aware of him?

But the audit needs to get behind mere fact or experience,
and ask the question on personal life and self-consciousness.
While each of these areas is concerned with the personal and

intimate details of a minister's life, and relationship with God, they cannot, to my mind, be excluded from any thorough ministerial appraisal. The Church runs the risk, at times, of adopting the models of such self-reflection from commerce and industry which have been shown to be questionable in their own fields.

That said, the need for self-reflection, with or without the help of another person or some sort of personality indicator, which in turn helps to nourish the inner self/relationship with God, seems self-evident. Each of us comes to ministry from a developed sense of working with God and with ourselves. How we can learn more about ourselves seems, therefore, to be of critical importance. The growth in usage of the Myers–Briggs Personality Type Indicator (MBTI) in both pre-selection and initial training in this country and the USA points to a growing need for some sort of tool to assist in that developing set of relationships, a need felt by the participants as much as by the institutions.

In his book *Holding in Trust*, Michael Jacobs rightly points out some of the inadequacies of such personality indicators, not least in the area that the 'choices' can be distorted by the user. Nonetheless, used over an extended period of time, the MBTI can provide some indication as to the preferred styles of action/being of the individual. The 'preferred' should, with guidance, lead us to the development of the secondary/shadow or, at best, the knowledge of how one is with oneself, and thus with others.

As one of our curates described the situation:

> knowing not only when I tick, but how I tick, and therefore when I'm not ticking helps me to understand the 'ticking of others'.

MBTI is about growth, the growth of the inner being/self from which everything else is derived. Chester and Norissey, in their book *Prayer and Temperament*, have developed the ideas of Myers–Briggs further by examining ways in which personality-type preferences may be parallelled in 'prayer typology'. While such a connection needs examination in our own culture, their thesis may prove to offer some way of handling the often juxtaposed understanding of ministerial appraisal vis-à-vis spiritual direction.

Talents and abilities lie, so often, unused for want of confidence, a lack of confidence which finds its root in not being valued by others or often not realizing that we are valued by God. Neither the audit nor an MBTI is a counsel of perfection, but an encouragement to a gentle self-remembrance.

God calls to ministry those who know their own hearts. For many, the way they are with themselves depends much on what they say or do. This damaging view of ministry which concentrates on skill, techniques and programmes prevents us from being in touch with the person whom God has created and seeks to sustain by his spirit. In being aware, gently, of ourselves, and thus of our own intimacy with God, we move away from a preoccupation with performance, towards the point at which we can begin to let God speak and work through us.

The perception often expressed by clergy is one of isolation/separation from the community both of the Church and of the world. Undoubtedly, the calling to ordination is much under threat today as the traditional values given by society to the role have been challenged. The concept of the person in the community, as the representative figure, no longer seems to hold true in many situations. The Church has become marginalized and has, in turn, looked inwards on itself, often as a means of self-protection. The minister has thus seen himself or herself as 'set apart', not in representational/focusing terms, but more in the felt experience of isolation. The urban-type chapter of clergy has created the need for defensiveness as a counter-balance to the pressure to be seen as successful at all costs.

For some, spiritual direction/guidance is sometimes seen as an alternative to ministerial review. The reality of many clergy's position would point to the value which such work can do in helping the individual to bring cohesion to what at times can easily become a disjointed life. It's worth noting, therefore, that spiritual direction cannot be carried out *within* the appraisal process but rather needs to be seen as a separate, but related, strand of one's development.

The way we are with others The personal thus leads us naturally to the consideration of the corporate 'The way we are with others'. Ordained some twenty years ago, I still remember the 'advice' of one pastoral tutor to 'avoid making friends in the parish for fear of creating division', advice which still seems to me to be a recipe for ministerial disaster. Clearly the choosing of favourites, like-minded people who collude with our own insecurities, is to be avoided at all costs but that is a long way from the mutual interrelatedness and openness which is pictured in the Gospels.

While Jesus spent time apart on the hill and in the desert, to be with his Father, the other side of his development was much influenced by an openness to others; an openness which was able to receive from those who opposed him as much as from those who responded to his message. Similarly, more recent Old Testament study has shown the false dichotomy which has hitherto been seen between the priest and the prophet. The prophet has been imagined as one who stands apart from the community, isolated, yet speaking words of correction to the life of the community. The priest, within the community of Israel, has been seen as someone who was unable to stand apart, being caught up in the cultic life of the community. New study has shown us that the prophet and the priest both live within the community of Israel and are supported and encouraged by that community as each seeks to develop his role under God. God calls individuals to be the means of calling the whole of his humanity to himself and to his Kingdom. While that call often left those who were called in positions of isolation, it was only when they were able to accept the support and encouragement of others that they were able to live out the call, both with regard to others and to the God who called:

> My friends, think what sort of people you are, whom God has called. Few of you are wise by any human standard, few powerful or of noble birth. Yet to shame the wise, God has chosen what the world counts folly, and to shame what is strong, God has chosen what the world counts weakness. He has chosen things without rank or standing in the world, mere nothings, to overthrow the existing order.
>
> (1 Corinthians 1.26–28)

In my experience appraisal, either by peer or outside consultant, as opposed to a work-centred, hierarchical model, highlights the need for clergy to develop what Edna Healey rightly describes as 'a hinterland of interest and relationships'. The peer/outside consultant model seems to give the participant the freedom to express the loneliness, the separation, which ministry often imposes upon the minister. The Corinthian passage to which I have referred reminds us that our response to the call of God can never be attempted in our own strength. Total dependence on God is required, as is also dependence upon those who would support us and encourage us in our ministry. We all know that our reaction to call is a sense of inadequacy; an inadequacy which is reinforced if we allow ourselves to be separated from others – the community of faith.

In looking at this area of 'The way we are with others', I am drawn back to the vocational work currently being undertaken by Francis Dewar. Dewar reminds us that the emphasis on the personal call of God to the individual is of recent origin within the life of the Church. Edward Schillebeeckx, in his book *Ministry: A Case for Change*, points out that in the first ten centuries of the Church's history, it was the local Christian community which had a major role to play in the choice of the leader. The unreal emphasis upon the inner call of God has led us to lose the sense of the corporate nature of the community which both calls and supports those whom it seeks to be the leaders of the community. Again, the pressures on clergy are all too often to leave the community behind, and that includes the everyday converse of friendship and interest, in seeking to fulfil the unrealistic expectation of being 'all things to all men and women'.

We also need to pay attention to the question as to whom we allow to share in our spiritual journey or, more importantly, who walks alongside us in that journey – for the way we are with others can never be separated from the way we are with God. Although in the past spiritual direction may have concentrated more upon the prayer life of the person, we need to recognize that the spiritual life or well-being of the individual is linked intimately with the whole person and the whole ministry. Much has been written on this subject, but let me refer to three books which might be useful:

> Gordon Jeff, *Spiritual Direction for Every Christian* (SPCK, London, 1987)
> Tilden Edwards, *Spiritual Friend* (New York, Paulist Press, 1980).
> Anne Long, *Approaches to Spiritual Direction* (Grove Booklets; Grove Books, Nottingham, 1984).

The development in recent years of spiritual direction right across the Churches, regardless of denomination or churchmanship, is something to be valued. Learning 'I cannot manage or develop on my own' seems to be a clue as to how spiritual direction and ministerial appraisal can lead to positive developments both for the individual and his or her ministry.

All that I have tried to say so far about ministry and spirituality is necessarily rooted in the way of our being with God. A life lived in connection with Christ should be our first and overriding concern. A life which is a life of prayer. Not prayer in the sense of prayers or rules of life, but a whole life which is prayerful.

The way we are with God If we are ever to bring others to the point of making the confession of faith it must surely be because in us they glimpse something of him who is the source and ground of life.

What, then, do we bring to that meeting point? Being involved with the discernment and selection of those who believe they are being called to the ordained ministry I meet, day by day, those who feel themselves rejected, The 'non-recommended', and those who sometimes believe that they have 'succeeded'. The use of such words as 'failure' and 'success' easily leads to the assumption that only those who bring a perfect wholeness to God are acceptable. The reality, as we all know, is far from that distorted view of the truth, yet it lies at the heart of much of the unease which clergy feel towards any appraisal system.

The emphasis on professionalism as a necessary mark of ministry needs to be seen alongside both the brokenness of those who seek to minister and the loving grace of him who both calls and strengthens us in our vocation. The call of God is to use everything which he has given us, but the emphasis must surely be upon the fact that it is God who calls, seeking to enter our lives and our relationships. If we are to ask ourselves: 'What do we bring to that meeting with God?', we must also ask ourselves: 'What kind of God do we know?' When we accept Christ as our Saviour we are immediately in a new relationship with God the Father:

> To prove that you are sons and daughters, God has sent into our hearts the spirit of his son, crying 'Abba! Father!'
>
> (Galatians 4)

So as we seek to re-engage with the God who first called us and healed us we need to remind ourselves that it is only by his grace and strength that we are able to offer him the brokenness and imperfection of our humanity. The offering which we make is one which we know is acceptable, precisely because he, as Creator, is responsible for that which he has created.

All too often, we seek to hold back from him that which we see as a possible barrier to his grace or even to those who through us would find in him life. Again, Dewar, in his book *Called or Collared*, points us to the need to increase our capacity to be open to God as he is, and to his loving invitation to each of us to offer ourselves and our energies so that others may flourish:

> But you must understand that in saying this I'm not talking about the God you say you believe in, the conscious beliefs of your intellect, which no doubt more or less correspond with credal orthodoxy. I am talking about the God that others might infer that you believe in, judging from your attitudes, the way you live your life, the type of person you are. That is the faith you actually live by, as opposed to the one you think you live by, and it can be quite difficult to be aware of, and even more difficult to change.

For many of us, our search for identity and purpose in ministry feels uncomfortable when the searchlight is placed upon our own prayer relationship with God. For many ministers, if not for most, the life of the Holy Spirit in revivifying and recreating is unknown territory. If we are to help others to grow in faith and relationship how can we do that if we have lost the vision, the presence of God, which first brought us to our moment of faith?

> 'Be still and know that I am God.' Psalm 46 reminds us that we are not only to be grounded in God but that we are to realise that in so placing ourselves we are acceptable to him i.e. that we have a self-worth which is God given and therefore a worth which we can accept for ourselves. Such being, as Augustine clearly recognised, helps us to be in touch with our deepest longing for God; but a longing which

is revealed to us in the knowledge that we are loved by him long before we were able to respond to that love.

Only when we spend time with God in silence and stillness can we truly become ministers, i.e. those who *minister* the 'things' of God to the people of God. Prayer thus becomes the vehicle through which the life-giving grace of God is poured out into his world.

In his book *The Living Reminder*, Henri Nouwen sums this action up:

> Such a way of living, united with God, implies that what counts is not our lives, but the life of Christ in us. Ultimately, it is Christ in us from whom healing comes. Only Christ can break through our human alienation and restore the broken connections with each other and with God.

'Restoring the broken connections' could well be the sub-title for a handbook on ministerial review/appraisal. The review seeks to make connections between the minister and his work, between the minister and the person, and ultimately between the minister and God. If such a review is to be a valuable tool for today's minister it must ensure also that the connection between ministry and spirituality is upheld. To fail to do so will be to strengthen the false idea that appraisal is merely about finding out how well the minister is faring with a variety of tasks.

The way we are with ourselves; the way we are with others; the way we are with God: these are certainly appraisal themes. But each, in its own way, points us back to the ground of our being, which is God who chooses not only to reveal himself to us in Jesus Christ but to call us to share in his reconciling work.

References

C.P. Michael and M.C. Norissey, *Prayer and Temperament* (The Open Door, Charlottesville, Virginia, 1984).

I. Briggs Myers and P.B. Myers, *Gifts Differing* (Consulting Psychologists, Palo Alto, California, 1980).

F. Dewar, *Called or Collared* (SPCK, London, 1991).

S. Evans, sermon.

M. Jacobs, *Holding in Trust* (New Library of Pastoral Care; SPCK, London, 1989).

J. Macquarrie, *Paths in Spirituality* (SCM, London, 1972).

H. Nouwen, *The Living Reminder* (Gill and Macmillan, Dublin, 1982).

E. Schillebeeckx, *Ministry: A Case for Change* (SCM, London, 1981).